Spectrum Test Prep

Grade 3

Test Preparation for:

Reading
Language
Math

Program Authors:
Dale Foreman
Alan C. Cohen
Jerome D. Kaplan
Ruth Mitchell

Copyright © 2001 McGraw-Hill Children's Publishing

Printed in the United States of America. All rights reserved. Except as permitted under the United States Copyright Act, no part of this publication may be reproduced or distributed in any form or by any means, or stored in a database or retrieval system, without prior written permission from the publisher.

Send all inquiries to: McGraw-Hill Children's Publishing • 3195 Wilson Drive NW • Grand Rapids, MI 49544

ISBN: 0-7696-3053-7

1 2 3 4 5 6 7 8 9 10 PHXBK 07 06 05 04 03 02

The McGraw·Hill Companies

Table of Contents

Introduction	4
A Message to Parents and Teachers	6
A Message to Students	7
How to Use This Book	8
Skills and Strategies	10
Test Prep in Reading	12
Vocabulary	13
Test Yourself	18
Reading Comprehension	21
Test Yourself	31
Name and Answer Sheet	36
Test Practice	38
Test Prep in Language	48
Language Mechanics	49
Test Yourself	53
Language Expression	56
Test Yourself	66
Spelling	72
Test Yourself	74
Study Skills	76
Test Yourself	79
Name and Answer Sheet	81
Test Practice	83
Test Prep in Math	94
Concepts	95
Test Yourself	101
Computation	104
Test Yourself	110
Applications	113
Test Yourself	125
Name and Answer Sheet	129
Test Practice	131
Answer Keys	140
Reading Progress Chart	145
Language Progress Chart	146
Math Progress Chart	147

Test Prep

The Program That Teaches Test-Taking Achievement

For over two decades, McGraw-Hill has helped students perform their best when taking standardized achievement tests. Over the years, we have identified the skills and strategies that students need to master the challenges of taking a standardized test. Becoming familiar with the test-taking experience can help ensure your child's success.

Test Prep covers all test skill areas

Test Prep contains the subject areas that are represented in the five major standardized tests. *Test Prep* will help your child prepare for the following tests:

- California Achievement Tests® (CAT/5)
- Comprehensive Tests of Basic Skills (CTBS/4)
- Iowa Tests of Basic Skills® (ITBS, Form K)
- Metropolitan Achievement Test (MAT/7)
- Stanford Achievement Test (SAT/9)

Test Prep provides strategies for success

Many students need special support when preparing to take a standardized test. *Test Prep* gives your child the opportunity to practice and become familiar with:

- General test content
- The test format
- Listening and following standard directions
- Working in structured settings
- Maintaining a silent, sustained effort
- Using test-taking strategies

Test Prep is comprehensive

Test Prep provides a complete presentation of the types of skills covered in standardized tests in a variety of formats. These formats are similar to those your child will encounter when testing. The subject areas covered in this book include:

- Reading
- Language
- Math

Test Prep gives students the practice they need

Each student lesson provides several components that help develop test-taking skills:

- An **Example,** with directions and sample test items
- A **Tips** feature, that gives test-taking strategies
- A **Practice** section, that helps students practice answering questions in each test format

Each book gives focused test practice that builds confidence:

- A **Test Yourself** lesson for each unit gives students the opportunity to apply what they have learned in the unit.
- A **Test Practice** section gives students the experience of a longer test-like situation.
- A **Progress Chart** allows students to note and record their own progress.

Test Prep is the first and most successful program ever developed to help students become familiar with the test-taking experience. *Test Prep* can help to build self-confidence, reduce test anxiety, and provide the opportunity for students to successfully show what they have learned.

A Message to Parents and Teachers:

- **Standardized tests: the yardstick for your child's future**

    Standardized testing is one of the cornerstones of American education. From its beginning in the early part of this century, standardized testing has gradually become the yardstick by which student performance is judged. For better or worse, your child's future will be determined in great part by how well he or she performs on the standardized test used by your school district.

- **Even good students can have trouble with testing**

    In general, standardized tests are well designed and carefully developed to assess students' abilities in a consistent and balanced manner. However, there are many factors that can hinder the performance of an individual student when testing. These might include test anxiety, unfamiliarity with the test's format, or failure to understand the directions.

    In addition, it is rare that students are taught all of the material that appears on a standardized test. This is because the curriculum of most schools does not directly match the content of the standardized test. There will certainly be overlap between what your child learns in school and how he or she is tested, but some materials will probably be unfamiliar.

- **Ready to Test will lend a helping hand**

    It is because of the shortcomings of the standardized testing process that *Test Prep* was developed. The lessons in the book were created after a careful analysis of the most popular achievement tests. The items, while different from those on the tests, reflect the types of material that your child will encounter when testing. Students who use *Test Prep* will also become familiar with the format of the most popular achievement tests. This learning experience will reduce anxiety and give your child the opportunity to do his or her best on the next standardized test.

We urge you to review with your child the Message to Students and the feature "How to Use This Book" on pages 8-9. The information on these pages will help your child to use this book and develop important test-taking skills. We are confident that following the recommendations in this book will help your child to earn a test score that accurately reflects his or her true ability.

A Message to Students:

Frequently in school you will be asked to take a standardized achievement test. This test will show how much you know compared to other students in your grade. Your score on a standardized achievement test will help your teachers plan your education. It will also give you and your parents an idea of what your learning strengths and weaknesses are.

This book will help you do your best on a standardized achievement test. It will show you what to expect on the test and will give you a chance to practice important reading and test-taking skills. Here are some suggestions you can follow to make the best use of *Test Prep*.

Plan for success
- You'll do your best if you begin studying and do one or two lessons in this book each week. If you only have a little bit of time before a test is given, you can do one or two lessons each day.
- Study a little bit at a time, no more than 30 minutes a day. If you can, choose the same time each day to study in a quiet place.
- Keep a record of your score on each lesson. The charts on pp. 145-147 of this book will help you do this.

On the day of the test . . .
- Get a good night's sleep the night before the test. Have a light breakfast and lunch to keep from feeling drowsy during the test.
- Use the tips you learned in *Test Prep*. The most important tips are to skip difficult items, take the best guess when you're unsure of the answer, and try all the items.
- Don't worry if you are a little nervous when you take an achievement test. This is a natural feeling and may even help you stay alert.

How to Use This Book

1 Getting Started

Read the directions carefully.

Do the Sample item(s).

Read the Tips.

2 Practice

Complete the Practice items.

Continue working until you reach a Stop sign.

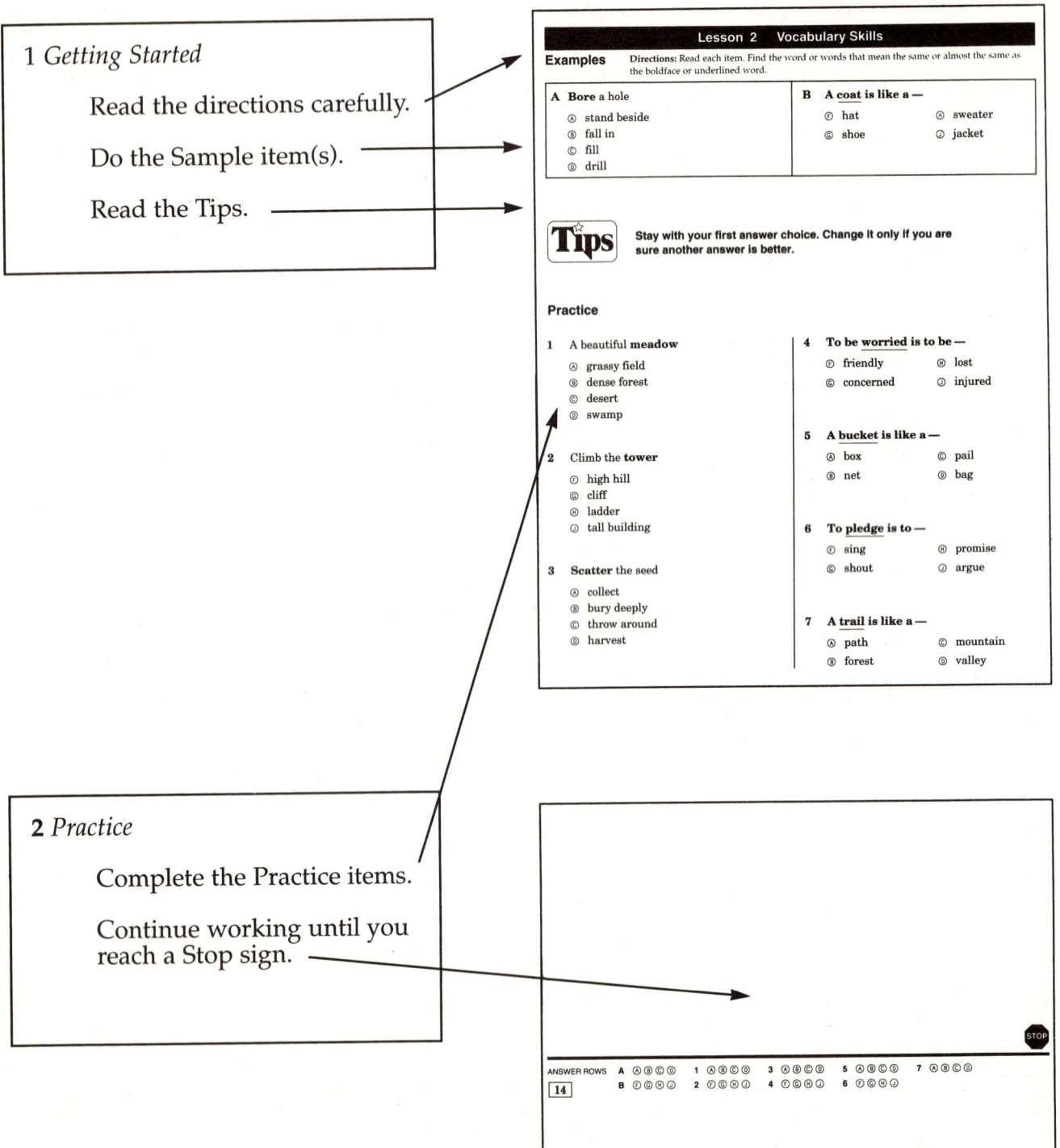

3 *Check It Out*

Check your answers by turning to the Answer Keys at the back of the book.

Keep track of how you're doing by marking the number right on the Progress Charts on pages 145-147.

Mark the lesson you completed on the Table of Contents for each section.

Answer Keys

Reading Unit 1, Vocabulary Lesson 1							
A	C	5	C	6	F	9	D
B	J	6	J	7	D	10	J
1	B	7	D	8	G	11	C
2	F	Lesson 6		Lesson 9		12	F
3	D	E1	C	1	B	13	C
4	H	E2	G	2	H	14	J
5	C	E3	C	3	A	15	A
6	J	1	D	4	J	16	J
7	D	2	F	5	B	17	C
Lesson 2		3	B	6	H	18	J
A	D	4	G	7	C	19	C
B	J	5	D	8	G	20	F
1	A	6	J	9	D	21	D
2	J	7	C	10	H	22	J
3	C	8	J	11	D	23	C
4	G	9	A	12	J	24	F
5	C	10	H	13	D	25	B
6	H	11	B	14	G	26	F
7	A	12	H	15	D	27	C
Lesson 3		13	C	16	G	28	G
A	B	14	F	17	A	Test Practice	
B	F	15	B	18	H	Part 2	
1	C	16	F	Lesson 10		E1	D
2	J	17	D	E1	C	1	C
3	D	18	F	1	C	2	G
4	F	19	C	2	J	3	D
5	C	20	F	3	A	4	G
6	G	21	B	4	F	5	D
7	C	22	J	5	B	6	F
28	F	23	A	6	J	7	C
Lesson 4		24	H	7	A	8	G
A	B	25	D	8	H	9	C
B	H	26	G	9	C	10	J
1	C	27	C	10	G	11	D
2	J	28	F	Test Practice		12	F
3	B	Unit 2, Reading Comprehension		Part 1		13	C
4	J	Lesson 7		E1	C	14	H
5	A	A	B	E2	G	15	B
Lesson 5		1	A	E3	D	16	F
A	C	2	H	1	A	17	B
B	G	3	D	2	J	18	G
1	B	Lesson 8		3	B	19	C
2	J	A	D	4	F	20	F
3	C	1	B	5	C	21	A
4	F	2	H	6	H	22	H
		3	C	7	B	23	D
		4	J	8	F	24	J
		5	B				

Reading Progress Chart
Circle your score for each lesson. Connect your scores to see how well you are doing.

Unit 1				Unit 2					
Lesson 1	Lesson 2	Lesson 3	Lesson 4	Lesson 5	Lesson 6	Lesson 7	Lesson 8	Lesson 9	Lesson 10
7	7	7	5	6	28	3	8	18	16
					27			17	15
					26			16	14
6	6	6	4	5	25 24 23 22 21	7	7	15 14 13	13 12
5	5	5		4	20 19 18	6	6	12 11	11 10
					17 16		5	10 9	9
4	4	4	3		15 14 13	2		9 8	8
3	3	3		3	12 11 10		4	8 7	7 6
			2		9 8 7	3	3	7 6 5	5 4
2	2	2		2	6 5 4	2	2	4 3	3 2
1	1	1	1	1	3 2 1	1	1	2 1	1

Table of Contents
Language

Unit 1   **Language Mechanics**

Lesson		Page
❏ 1	Capitalization	49
❏ 2	Punctuation	50
❏ 3	Capitalization and Punctuation	51
❏ 4	Test Yourself	53

Unit 2   **Language Expression**

Lesson		Page
❏ 5	Nouns and Pronouns	56
❏ 6	Verbs	58
❏ 7	Adjectives	59
❏ 8	Sentences	60
❏ 9	Paragraphs	63
❏ 10	Test Yourself	66

Unit 3   **Spelling**

Lesson		Page
❏ 11	Spelling Skills	72
❏ 12	Test Yourself	74

Unit 4   **Study Skills**

Lesson		Page
❏ 13	Study Skills	76
❏ 14	Test Yourself	79
❏	Name and Answer Sheet	81

Unit 5   **Test Practice**

Part		Page
❏ 1	Language Mechanics	83
❏ 2	Language Expression	86
❏ 3	Spelling	90
❏ 4	Study Skills	92

Skills

Reading

VOCABULARY

Identifying synonyms
Identifying words with similar meanings
Identifying antonyms
Identifying multi-meaning words
Identifying words from a defining statement

READING COMPREHENSION

Recognizing story structures
Differentiating between fact and opinion
Making comparisons
Identifying story genres
Recognizing details
Understanding events
Drawing conclusions
Applying story information
Deriving word or phrase meaning
Understanding characters
Recognizing a narrator
Sequencing ideas
Making inferences
Labeling pictures
Generalizing from story information
Predicting from story content
Choosing the best title for a passage
Referring to a graphic
Understanding the author's purpose
Understanding feelings
Understanding the main idea

Language

LANGUAGE MECHANICS

Identifying the need for capital letters (proper nouns, beginning words) in sentences
Identifying the need for capital letters and punctuation marks in printed text
Identifying the need for punctuation marks (period, question mark, apostrophe, comma) in sentences

LANGUAGE EXPRESSION

Identifying the correct forms of nouns and pronouns
Identifying the correct forms of adjectives
Identifying correctly formed sentences
Sequencing sentences within a paragraph
Identifying the subject of a sentence
Combining sentences
Identifying the correct sentence to complete a paragraph
Identifying the predicate of a sentence
Identifying the correct forms of verbs
Identifying sentences that do not fit in a paragraph

SPELLING

Identifying correctly spelled words
Identifying incorrectly spelled words

MATH

CONCEPTS

Recognizing ordinal position
Comparing and ordering whole numbers
Comparing sets
Sequencing numbers
Renaming numerals
Understanding place value
Recognizing fractional parts
Using expanded notation
Using a number line
Grouping by 10s
Recognizing numerals
Skip counting by 10s
Recognizing visual and numeric patterns
Identifying fractions

Comparing and ordering fractions
Using operational symbols, words, and properties
Rounding
Recognizing odd and even numbers
Regrouping
Estimating

COMPUTATION

Adding whole numbers, decimals, and fractions
Dividing whole numbers
Multiplying whole numbers
Subtracting whole numbers, decimals, and fractions

APPLICATIONS

Finding perimeter and area
Solving word problems
Reading a calendar
Reading a thermometer
Recognizing plane and solid figures and their characteristics
Recognizing value of coins, bills, and money notation
Telling time
Identifying information needed to solve a problem
Estimating weight, size, and temperature
Understanding elapsed time
Understanding congruence, symmetry, and line segments
Understanding bar graphs, pictographs, and tables

Strategies

Listening carefully
Following group directions
Utilizing test formats
Locating question and answer choices
Following oral directions
Subvocalizing answer choices
Recalling information about word structure
Skipping difficult items and returning to them later
Identifying and using key words to find the answer
Staying with the first answer
Analyzing answer choices
Trying out answer choices
Eliminating answer choices
Restating a question
Substituting answer choices
Using logic
Using sentence context to find the answer
Referring to a passage to find the correct answer
Indicating that an item has no mistakes
Evaluating answer choices
Recalling the elements of a correctly formed sentence
Converting problems to a workable format
Noting the lettering of answer choices
Taking the best guess when unsure of the answer
Indicating that the correct answer is not given
Identifying the best test-taking strategy
Locating the correct answer
Comparing answer choices
Marking the correct answer as soon as it is found

Adjusting to a structured setting
Maintaining a silent, sustained effort
Managing time effectively
Considering every answer choice
Computing carefully
Working methodically
Using context to find the answer
Locating the correct answer
Understanding unusual item formats
Following complex directions
Inferring word meaning from sentence context
Reasoning from facts and evidence
Encapsulating a passage
Skimming a passage
Avoiding over-analysis of answer choices
Recalling the function of verbs
Noting the differences among answer choices
Referring to a reference source
Recalling the elements of a correctly formed paragraph
Checking answers by the opposite operation
Finding the answer without computing
Performing the correct operation
Understanding oral questions
Identifying and using key words, figures, and numbers
Following written directions
Reworking a problem
Previewing items

Table of Contents
Reading

Unit 1 **Vocabulary**

Lesson		Page
❑ 1	Synonyms	13
❑ 2	Vocabulary Skills	14
❑ 3	Antonyms	15
❑ 4	Multi-Meaning Words	16
❑ 5	Words in Context	17
❑ 6	Test Yourself	18

Unit 2 **Reading Comprehension**

Lesson		Page
❑ 7	Critical Reading	21
❑ 8	Literal Comprehension	22
❑ 9	Inferential Comprehension	25
❑ 10	Test Yourself	31
❑	Name and Answer Sheet	36

Unit 3 **Test Practice**

Part		Page
❑ 1	Vocabulary	38
❑ 2	Reading Comprehension	41

UNIT 1 VOCABULARY

Lesson 1 Synonyms

Examples **Directions:** Read each item. Find the word that means the same or almost the same as the underlined word.

A costly ticket

- Ⓐ distant
- Ⓑ ordinary
- Ⓒ expensive
- Ⓓ winning

B I felt clumsy when I went skiing.

- Ⓕ tired
- Ⓖ graceful
- Ⓗ frightened
- Ⓙ awkward

 If you aren't sure of the answer, replace the underlined word with each answer choice and say the phrase to yourself.

Practice

1 search beneath
- Ⓐ beside
- Ⓑ below
- Ⓒ above
- Ⓓ along

2 free the animal
- Ⓕ release
- Ⓖ harm
- Ⓗ attract
- Ⓙ search

3 sometimes injure
- Ⓐ help
- Ⓑ carry
- Ⓒ miss
- Ⓓ hurt

4 view the scene
- Ⓕ leave
- Ⓖ enjoy
- Ⓗ observe
- Ⓙ purchase

5 Ellen's coat was ruined.
- Ⓐ cleaned
- Ⓑ repaired
- Ⓒ destroyed
- Ⓓ lost

6 The dry leaves were brittle.
- Ⓕ noisy
- Ⓖ damp
- Ⓗ colorful
- Ⓙ fragile

7 What do you do with stale bread?
- Ⓐ fresh
- Ⓑ old
- Ⓒ warm
- Ⓓ toasted

ANSWER ROWS **A** Ⓐ Ⓑ Ⓒ Ⓓ   **1** Ⓐ Ⓑ Ⓒ Ⓓ   **3** Ⓐ Ⓑ Ⓒ Ⓓ   **5** Ⓐ Ⓑ Ⓒ Ⓓ   **7** Ⓐ Ⓑ Ⓒ Ⓓ
              B Ⓕ Ⓖ Ⓗ Ⓙ   **2** Ⓕ Ⓖ Ⓗ Ⓙ   **4** Ⓕ Ⓖ Ⓗ Ⓙ   **6** Ⓕ Ⓖ Ⓗ Ⓙ

13

Lesson 2 Vocabulary Skills

Examples Directions: Read each item. Find the word or words that mean the same or almost the same as the boldface or underlined word.

A **Bore** a hole
- Ⓐ stand beside
- Ⓑ fall in
- Ⓒ fill
- Ⓓ drill

B A <u>coat</u> is like a —
- Ⓕ hat
- Ⓖ shoe
- Ⓗ sweater
- Ⓙ jacket

 **Tips** Stay with your first answer choice. Change it only if you are sure another answer is better.

Practice

1 A beautiful **meadow**
- Ⓐ grassy field
- Ⓑ dense forest
- Ⓒ desert
- Ⓓ swamp

2 Climb the **tower**
- Ⓕ high hill
- Ⓖ cliff
- Ⓗ ladder
- Ⓙ tall building

3 **Scatter** the seed
- Ⓐ collect
- Ⓑ bury deeply
- Ⓒ throw around
- Ⓓ harvest

4 To be <u>worried</u> is to be —
- Ⓕ friendly
- Ⓖ concerned
- Ⓗ lost
- Ⓙ injured

5 A <u>bucket</u> is like a —
- Ⓐ box
- Ⓑ net
- Ⓒ pail
- Ⓓ bag

6 To <u>pledge</u> is to —
- Ⓕ sing
- Ⓖ shout
- Ⓗ promise
- Ⓙ argue

7 A <u>trail</u> is like a —
- Ⓐ path
- Ⓑ forest
- Ⓒ mountain
- Ⓓ valley

ANSWER ROWS
A Ⓐ Ⓑ Ⓒ Ⓓ   1 Ⓐ Ⓑ Ⓒ Ⓓ   3 Ⓐ Ⓑ Ⓒ Ⓓ   5 Ⓐ Ⓑ Ⓒ Ⓓ   7 Ⓐ Ⓑ Ⓒ Ⓓ
B Ⓕ Ⓖ Ⓗ Ⓙ   2 Ⓕ Ⓖ Ⓗ Ⓙ   4 Ⓕ Ⓖ Ⓗ Ⓙ   6 Ⓕ Ⓖ Ⓗ Ⓙ

Lesson 3   Antonyms

Examples   **Directions:** Read each item. Choose the word that means the opposite of the underlined word.

A Caitlin will <u>toss</u> the ball first.
- Ⓐ hit
- Ⓑ catch
- Ⓒ throw
- Ⓓ find

B buy <u>some</u>
- Ⓕ none
- Ⓖ several
- Ⓗ that
- Ⓙ cheap

Remember, you are looking for the answer that means the <u>opposite</u> of the underlined word.

Practice

1 Stony was <u>pleased</u> with his score.
- Ⓐ happy
- Ⓑ unsure
- Ⓒ annoyed
- Ⓓ satisfied

2 I <u>stretched</u> my sweater.
- Ⓕ lost
- Ⓖ washed
- Ⓗ found
- Ⓙ shrank

3 The train ride was <u>jerky</u>.
- Ⓐ long
- Ⓑ enjoyable
- Ⓒ bumpy
- Ⓓ smooth

4 work <u>slowly</u>
- Ⓕ rapidly
- Ⓖ harshly
- Ⓗ kindly
- Ⓙ soon

5 <u>recent</u> newspaper
- Ⓐ delivered
- Ⓑ thick
- Ⓒ old
- Ⓓ expensive

6 was <u>furious</u>
- Ⓕ angry
- Ⓖ calm
- Ⓗ curious
- Ⓙ uncertain

7 <u>except</u> Randy
- Ⓐ like
- Ⓑ with
- Ⓒ including
- Ⓓ despite

ANSWER ROWS A Ⓐ Ⓑ Ⓒ Ⓓ   1 Ⓐ Ⓑ Ⓒ Ⓓ   3 Ⓐ Ⓑ Ⓒ Ⓓ   5 Ⓐ Ⓑ Ⓒ Ⓓ   7 Ⓐ Ⓑ Ⓒ Ⓓ
             B Ⓕ Ⓖ Ⓗ Ⓙ   2 Ⓕ Ⓖ Ⓗ Ⓙ   4 Ⓕ Ⓖ Ⓗ Ⓙ   6 Ⓕ Ⓖ Ⓗ Ⓙ

Lesson 4 Multi-Meaning Words

Examples Directions: For items A and 1-3, read the two sentences with the blanks. Choose the word that fits both sentences. For items B and 4-5, find the answer in which the underlined word is used the same as in the sentence in the box.

A We looked in both _____ .

What do the _____ say?

- Ⓐ paths
- Ⓑ directions
- Ⓒ words
- Ⓓ boxes

B | The park is crowded today. |

In which sentence does the word park mean the same thing as in the sentence above?

- Ⓕ Where did you park the car?
- Ⓖ You will learn to park soon.
- Ⓗ The children played in the park.
- Ⓙ Park beside the supermarket.

Tips Watch out! Only one answer is correct in both sentences or matches the meaning of the sentence in the box.

Practice

1 Rosa paid a library _____ .
The carpenter did a _____ job.

- Ⓐ fee
- Ⓑ good
- Ⓒ fine
- Ⓓ great

2 Let's take a _____ now.
Did Randy _____ his skateboard?

- Ⓕ rest
- Ⓖ lose
- Ⓗ find
- Ⓙ break

3 Loren got a _____ for her work.
Be sure to _____ the dog's water.

- Ⓐ fee
- Ⓑ check
- Ⓒ fill
- Ⓓ reward

4 | Shara hurt her hand yesterday. |

In which sentence does the word hand mean the same thing as in the sentence above?

- Ⓕ Please hand me that bowl.
- Ⓖ The crowd gave the player a hand.
- Ⓗ On one hand, they did their best.
- Ⓙ Put your hand under the bag.

5 | In general, it was a good play. |

In which sentence does the word general mean the same thing as in the sentence above?

- Ⓐ He made a general comment about the food.
- Ⓑ The general will arrive soon.
- Ⓒ The small town had a general store.
- Ⓓ Lucy's mother is a general.

Lesson 5 Words in Context

Examples **Directions:** For items A and 1-3, read the paragraph or sentence. Find the word below that fits best in the blanks. For items B and 4-6, read the sentence with the underlined word. Find the word below that means the same or almost the same as the underlined word.

A The children helped their parents _____ the family car. They used the garden hose for water.

- Ⓐ buy
- Ⓑ repair
- Ⓒ wash
- Ⓓ sell

B Many people visited the famous museum in our town. Famous means —

- Ⓕ large
- Ⓖ well-known
- Ⓗ science
- Ⓙ old-fashioned

 Use the meaning of the sentence to decide which answer choice is correct.

Practice

1 The test was _____, but I did well.

Find the word that means the test was not easy.

- Ⓐ silent
- Ⓑ difficult
- Ⓒ short
- Ⓓ simple

The rain __(2)__ against the window. The thunder boomed and the __(3)__ flashed.

2
- Ⓕ attended
- Ⓖ gushed
- Ⓗ wet
- Ⓙ pounded

3
- Ⓐ storm
- Ⓑ weather
- Ⓒ lightning
- Ⓓ wind

4 The _____ cabin withstood the storm.

Which word means the cabin was strong?

- Ⓕ sturdy
- Ⓖ weak
- Ⓗ cozy
- Ⓙ huge

5 Are you allowed to go with us? Allowed means —

- Ⓐ happy
- Ⓑ excited
- Ⓒ permitted
- Ⓓ ready

6 A safety zone surrounded the chemical plant. Zone means —

- Ⓕ fence
- Ⓖ road
- Ⓗ lake
- Ⓙ area

ANSWER ROWS A Ⓐ Ⓑ Ⓒ Ⓓ   1 Ⓐ Ⓑ Ⓒ Ⓓ   3 Ⓐ Ⓑ Ⓒ Ⓓ   5 Ⓐ Ⓑ Ⓒ Ⓓ
            B Ⓕ Ⓖ Ⓗ Ⓙ   2 Ⓕ Ⓖ Ⓗ Ⓙ   4 Ⓕ Ⓖ Ⓗ Ⓙ   6 Ⓕ Ⓖ Ⓗ Ⓙ

Lesson 6   Test Yourself

Examples   **Directions:** Read the phrase with the underlined word. Find the word below that means the same or almost the same as the underlined word.

E1 <u>rely</u> on her
- Ⓐ breathe
- Ⓑ watch
- Ⓒ depend
- Ⓓ stand

E2 <u>accept</u> a job
- Ⓕ take
- Ⓖ reject
- Ⓗ seek
- Ⓙ realize

1 sunshine is <u>likely</u>
- Ⓐ enjoyable
- Ⓑ rare
- Ⓒ impossible
- Ⓓ probable

2 <u>cancel</u> an order
- Ⓕ stop
- Ⓖ give
- Ⓗ make
- Ⓙ extend

3 happen <u>frequently</u>
- Ⓐ quickly
- Ⓑ often
- Ⓒ occasionally
- Ⓓ now

4 How can we <u>attach</u> this?
- Ⓕ separate
- Ⓖ connect
- Ⓗ repair
- Ⓙ examine

5 The house on the lake was <u>lovely</u>.
- Ⓐ run-down
- Ⓑ lonely
- Ⓒ small
- Ⓓ charming

6 <u>Rare</u> coins
- Ⓕ cheap
- Ⓖ beautiful
- Ⓗ damaged
- Ⓙ unusual

7 <u>Inspect</u> the food
- Ⓐ freeze
- Ⓑ carry
- Ⓒ check carefully
- Ⓓ cook well

8 A <u>bundle</u> is a —
- Ⓕ friend
- Ⓖ mistake
- Ⓗ newspaper
- Ⓙ package

9 To <u>soar</u> is to —
- Ⓐ fly high
- Ⓑ sink quickly
- Ⓒ run around
- Ⓓ follow closely

Lesson 6 Test Yourself

Directions: For numbers 10-14, read the phrase with the underlined word. Find the word below that means the opposite of the underlined word.

10 Those fish are very <u>colorful</u>.
- Ⓕ bright
- Ⓖ large
- Ⓗ strange
- Ⓙ dull

11 People <u>often</u> visit this beach.
- Ⓐ frequently
- Ⓑ rarely
- Ⓒ usually
- Ⓓ happily

12 The path to the lake is <u>straight</u> for about a mile.
- Ⓕ narrow
- Ⓖ wide
- Ⓗ crooked
- Ⓙ dangerous

13 feeling <u>excited</u>
- Ⓐ frightened
- Ⓒ calm
- Ⓑ angry
- Ⓓ nervous

14 <u>either</u> road
- Ⓕ neither
- Ⓗ broad
- Ⓖ that
- Ⓙ which

Directions: For numbers 15-16, find the word that fits in both sentences. For 17 and 18, find the answer in which the underlined word is used the same as in the sentence in the box.

15 Is _____ meat better for you?

Don't _____ against the paint.
- Ⓐ fresh
- Ⓑ lean
- Ⓒ fall
- Ⓓ cheap

16 She got water from the _____ .

Are you feeling _____ ?
- Ⓕ well
- Ⓖ bottle
- Ⓗ sick
- Ⓙ hungry

17 Remember to <u>sign</u> your name.

In which sentence does the word sign mean the same thing as in the sentence above?
- Ⓐ The <u>sign</u> blew down in the storm.
- Ⓑ Robins are a sure <u>sign</u> of spring.
- Ⓒ A small <u>sign</u> showed the way to the inn.
- Ⓓ Did you <u>sign</u> the form yet?

18 How long will the storm <u>last</u>?

In which sentence does the word last mean the same thing as in the sentence above?
- Ⓕ The movie will <u>last</u> until nine o'clock.
- Ⓖ Is this the <u>last</u> orange?
- Ⓗ The <u>last</u> part of the story is the best.
- Ⓙ Rudy moved here <u>last</u> year.

GO

19

Lesson 6   Test Yourself

Directions: For items 19-28, read the sentences, then find the answer that fits best in the blank in the sentence or means the same as an underlined word.

19 Jasmine wanted to _____ the offer.

Find the word that means Jasmine wanted to think about the offer.

- Ⓐ exceed
- Ⓒ consider
- Ⓑ dismiss
- Ⓓ align

20 Thick beams _____ the roof.

Which word means the beams held the roof up?

- Ⓕ supported
- Ⓗ formed
- Ⓖ weighed
- Ⓙ aligned

21 The horse <u>approached</u> the fence. <u>Approached</u> means —

- Ⓐ retreated
- Ⓒ jumped over
- Ⓑ came near
- Ⓓ beyond

22 Do you <u>recall</u> who said that? <u>Recall</u> means —

- Ⓕ replace
- Ⓗ forget
- Ⓖ dislike
- Ⓙ remember

The __(23)__ of the country went on strike. They wanted the __(24)__ to treat them more fairly.

23
- Ⓐ citizens
- Ⓒ enemies
- Ⓑ voices
- Ⓓ creatures

24
- Ⓕ friend
- Ⓗ ruler
- Ⓖ manager
- Ⓙ register

T.J.'s family took a __(25)__ vacation. It was a __(26)__ trip that lasted a month and included a raft trip down the Colorado River.

25
- Ⓐ minor
- Ⓒ single
- Ⓑ plain
- Ⓓ lengthy

26
- Ⓕ certain
- Ⓗ refunded
- Ⓖ wonderful
- Ⓙ profitable

The price of shoes was __(27)__ because of a holiday sale. Marnie __(28)__ to buy tennis and running shoes.

27
- Ⓐ increased
- Ⓒ reduced
- Ⓑ unchanged
- Ⓓ lost

28
- Ⓕ decided
- Ⓗ loaded
- Ⓖ avoided
- Ⓙ rested

UNIT 2 READING COMPREHENSION

Lesson 7 Critical Reading

Examples **Directions:** Read each item. Choose the answer you think is correct. Mark the space for your answer.

Yesterday morning, the governor signed the bill that will set aside five million dollars to improve state parks and hire school students to work in the parks during the summer.

A This sentence would most likely be found in a —

- Ⓐ biography.
- Ⓑ newspaper article.
- Ⓒ fairy tale.
- Ⓓ mystery.

 If a question seems confusing, try restating it to yourself in simpler terms.

Practice

1 Arnold is reading a story called "The Dream of Space Travel". Which of these sentences would most likely be at the very end of the story?

- Ⓐ The dream has not come true, but it might in the near future.
- Ⓑ Before the first plane was invented, people dreamed of space travel.
- Ⓒ Rockets were invented by the Chinese almost 1000 years ago.
- Ⓓ Stories of travel through the heavens are told in many cultures.

2 Which of these would most likely be found in a mystery story?

- Ⓕ The President lives in Washington.
- Ⓖ Bears eat many different foods.
- Ⓗ Dolores opened the door slowly, but no one was there.
- Ⓙ Before you can fix a leaky roof, you must find the leak.

3 A student is reading this story about the West.

The wagon train stopped for the night. Nan and Marty unhitched the horses and tied them to a nearby tree. The horses had fresh grass to eat and cold water to drink from a spring.

Which sentence is most likely to come next?

- Ⓐ It was morning, and there was much to do before they could start out.
- Ⓑ The first horses were brought to America by Spanish explorers.
- Ⓒ The cottonwood tree made a strange shadow in the moonlight.
- Ⓓ The two children hurried back to the wagon to help prepare dinner.

STOP

ANSWER ROW   A Ⓐ Ⓑ Ⓒ Ⓓ   1 Ⓐ Ⓑ Ⓒ Ⓓ   2 Ⓕ Ⓖ Ⓗ Ⓙ   3 Ⓐ Ⓑ Ⓒ Ⓓ   21

Lesson 8   Literal Comprehension

Examples   Directions: Read each passage. Choose the best answer for each question that follows the passage.

"Have you seen my shoes?" "No. Didn't you leave them on the porch because they were muddy?" "I guess I did. I'll look there now. Don't leave without me."	A These people are probably — Ⓐ coming home Ⓑ resting Ⓒ arguing Ⓓ going out

 Skim the story and then read the questions. Refer back to the story to answer the questions.

Practice

"Do you hear something, Magda?"

"It sounds like a cat. Where could the noise be coming from?"

Magda and Mr. Howard went outside and looked to see what the noise was. They couldn't find anything. They looked under the car and behind the trash cans.

"Let's go back in, Magda. We can look around later if we hear the sound again."

"I want to look under the bush. Then I'll come in."

Magda crawled way under the bush beside the house. It was dark and she couldn't see very well. Just then, something furry crawled up against her face. Magda almost jumped out of her skin! It was a kitten, and it started licking her.

"Dad! Dad! Remember when you said I could have a kitten? I think my kitten just found me."

1   **A bush is a kind of plant. Find another word that is a kind of plant.**

Ⓐ rock   Ⓑ tree   Ⓒ garden

2   **What caused Magda to "almost jump out of her skin"?**

Ⓕ She heard something under the bush.

Ⓖ She wanted a kitten.

Ⓗ Something furry crawled up against her.

22

ANSWER ROW   A Ⓐ Ⓑ Ⓒ Ⓓ   1 Ⓐ Ⓑ Ⓒ   2 Ⓕ Ⓖ Ⓗ

Lesson 8   Literal Comprehension

"Mom, there's nothing to do. I'm bored."

"Why, Reggie, how can that be? We live in one of the biggest cities in the world. There are a million things for you to do. Why don't you walk down to the park?"

"That's really boring. Can I go over to Alida's? Aunt Millie said it's okay."

"That's a good idea. But go right over to the apartment. Don't stop in the video arcade like you usually do. I'll call Aunt Millie in about twenty minutes to check up on you."

Reggie grabbed his coat and hat and ran out the door and down the steps. He waited for the light to change, looked both ways, and crossed the street. There was always a lot of traffic on the street outside his apartment building, and he didn't want to get hit by a car.

He ran into the park and followed the path that went by the lake. Alida and her family lived on the other side of the park. Their apartment was almost a mile away, and he didn't want to waste time and worry his mother.

As Reggie passed the lake, he saw the strangest thing. A crowd of people was gathered around watching pirates row an old-fashioned boat on the lake!

Although he knew he should go right over to Alida's apartment, Reggie couldn't resist joining the crowd of people by the lake. When he got closer, he saw lots of lights, some cameras, and some people shouting orders at the pirates. It was very exciting, especially when the pirates got into a sword fight. None of them got hurt, of course, but one of them fell into the lake. Everyone got a good laugh at that.

After about ten minutes, Reggie suddenly remembered what he was supposed to be doing. He turned away from the crowd and started running down the path. If he hurried, he would still get to Alida's apartment before his mother called.

Lesson 8   Literal Comprehension

3 **Where do you think Reggie lives?**

Ⓐ On a quiet street

Ⓑ Near a river

Ⓒ On a busy street

Ⓓ Near the ocean

4 **Which of these statements is probably true about Reggie?**

Ⓕ He never does what his mother says.

Ⓖ His sister's name is Alida.

Ⓗ He often jogs in the park.

Ⓙ He likes to play video games.

5 **What made Reggie stop at the lake on his way to Alida's?**

Ⓐ Students who were practicing for a school play

Ⓑ A crowd watching pirates

Ⓒ Real pirates in the park

Ⓓ Some people getting ready for Halloween

6 **About how long does it usually take to get to Alida's apartment?**

Ⓕ Less than twenty minutes

Ⓖ More than twenty minutes

Ⓗ About five minutes

Ⓙ About thirty minutes

7 **What made Reggie remember what he was supposed to do?**

Ⓐ The sword fight

Ⓑ Seeing someone fall in the lake

Ⓒ Someone in the crowd

Ⓓ The story doesn't say.

8 **When he gets to Alida's house, Reggie will probably —**

Ⓕ make up a story explaining why he was late.

Ⓖ explain what happened in the park.

Ⓗ look for something to eat.

Ⓙ ask Alida what happened in the park that day.

ANSWER ROWS   3 Ⓐ Ⓑ Ⓒ Ⓓ   5 Ⓐ Ⓑ Ⓒ Ⓓ   7 Ⓐ Ⓑ Ⓒ Ⓓ
              4 Ⓕ Ⓖ Ⓗ Ⓙ   6 Ⓕ Ⓖ Ⓗ Ⓙ   8 Ⓕ Ⓖ Ⓗ Ⓙ

Lesson 9   Inferential Comprehension

Examples   **Directions:** Read the passage. Find the best answer to each question that follows the passage.

Robbie got up early without anyone waking him. Today, he and the rest of the family were going fishing at Parker Lake. Robbie loved fishing, and Parker Lake had the best fishing around. They were going to rent a boat and spend the whole day on the lake. He was sure he would catch a big one.	A How do you think Robbie feels? Ⓐ Worried Ⓑ Proud Ⓒ Excited Ⓓ Disappointed

   Look for key words in the question and the answer choices. They will help you find the correct answer.

Practice

Why should people drink milk?

Humans have probably been drinking milk for as long as they have been on earth. People who study the history of the world have found pictures from long, long ago that show people milking cows and using the milk for food.

Milk is the first food of babies. Animals that produce milk to feed their babies are called mammals. Their mother's milk is usually the best food for all young mammals.

The milk that people in America drink every day comes from cows, although many people prefer to drink the milk of goats. These two animals produce more milk than what their own babies need, and farmers collect the milk to sell it. In other countries, people also drink the milk of camels, horses, yaks, reindeer, sheep, and water buffaloes.

Milk is sometimes called the most nearly perfect food. It contains many of the things that humans need for healthy bodies, such as calcium, phosphorous, and protein. Milk also has several necessary vitamins and is easily digested by most humans. Another reason milk is such a good food is because some of its ingredients are found nowhere else in nature.

The one problem milk has is that it contains a lot of animal fat. This is good for young children, but not for adults. Foods with too much fat cause adults to have heart disease. Sometimes the fatty part of milk, the cream, is removed. This milk is called low-fat milk or skim milk. The cream that is removed from the milk is used to make ice cream and other foods. Milk is also used to make butter, cheese, and other dairy foods that people enjoy.

Besides being an important food, milk also provides chemicals that can be turned into other products. These chemicals are used to make paint, glue, cloth, and plastic.

1 Which phrase from the story describes how good milk is?

- Ⓐ ...the first food of babies...
- Ⓑ ...the most nearly perfect...
- Ⓒ ...easily digested by most humans...
- Ⓓ ...other dairy foods...

2 Milk is used for all of these things except—

- Ⓕ butter.
- Ⓖ fabric for clothing.
- Ⓗ paint for a house.
- Ⓙ automobile tires.

3 Look at the picture on page 25. The picture shows the children —

- Ⓐ drinking milk.
- Ⓑ eating something.
- Ⓒ waiting for someone.
- Ⓓ playing a game.

4 Most of the milk that we drink comes from—

- Ⓕ wild animals.
- Ⓖ big cities.
- Ⓗ yaks and water buffaloes.
- Ⓙ farm animals.

5 Which of these would be best for an adult?

- Ⓐ Ice cream
- Ⓑ Low-fat milk
- Ⓒ Butter
- Ⓓ Regular milk

6 What is a word from the story that means "something made from other things"?

- Ⓕ Ingredient
- Ⓖ Necessary
- Ⓗ Product
- Ⓙ Dairy

Graceful and Strong

Maria Tallchief was one of the most famous ballet dancers in the world. When she performed, the people in the audience loved to watch her dance. She was so graceful and so strong that she made the dancing look easy.

Born on an Osage Indian reservation in Oklahoma, Tallchief was given the name Betty Marie. Her mother thought the girl had special talents and tried to encourage them. When she was three, Tallchief began taking piano lessons. The next year, she started dance lessons even though most girls are not ready to start ballet until they are seven or eight years old. The young Tallchief did well in both piano and ballet.

Betty Marie's family moved to California so she and her sister could have more lessons. Betty Marie's teacher told her that a ballet dancer has to train harder than an athlete who plays football or baseball. Dance can be more challenging than any other sport, and Betty Marie worked as hard as she could.

Soon, Betty Marie's teachers told her she had to choose between ballet and piano. It was the only way she could develop her talent. She enjoyed both, but decided that she loved ballet more. When she was a teenager, she joined a Russian ballet group and changed her name. She thought Maria sounded more like a Russian name. She did not give up her Indian name, Tallchief.

Maria loved dancing, and people loved to watch her dance. She became famous all over the world. When Tallchief visited her home state of Oklahoma, the Osage Indian tribe made her a princess and performed Indian dances in her honor.

Tallchief continued to travel and dance, but she did not like being away from her family, especially her child. She stopped dancing to stay at home with her daughter. Later, Maria Tallchief started a ballet school to help other talented youngsters develop their dance skills. She wanted other girls to love ballet as much as she did.

7 Maria Tallchief's two talents in childhood were ___ and ___.

Ⓐ Singing and dancing.
Ⓑ Playing piano and singing.
Ⓒ Dancing and playing piano.
Ⓓ Acting and singing.

8 Which of these is an opinion in the story?

Ⓕ The Osage Indian reservation is in Oklahoma.
Ⓖ People loved to watch Maria Tallchief dance.
Ⓗ Maria Tallchief started a ballet school for young dancers.
Ⓙ Maria Tallchief changed her first name but would not change her last name.

9 You can tell from reading this selection that ballet dancers must be—

Ⓐ beautiful and very smart.
Ⓑ able to play the piano very well.
Ⓒ tall and have long hair.
Ⓓ strong and willing to work hard.

10 At different times in her life, Maria had to make hard choices. She gave up all of these things except one. What did she **not** give up?

Ⓕ Playing piano
Ⓖ Her family
Ⓗ Ballet
Ⓙ The name Betty Marie

11 Why did the Tallchief family move from Oklahoma to California?

Ⓐ To live with relatives
Ⓑ So Betty Marie's father could get a better job
Ⓒ To give Betty Marie a chance to change her name
Ⓓ So Betty Marie could have better ballet lessons

12 Betty Marie's teacher compares ballet to —

Ⓕ sports that are easy.
Ⓖ games that are fun.
Ⓗ playing a musical instrument.
Ⓙ sports that require hard work.

An Elephant Grows Up

Sikar was a 7-year-old male elephant. He had lived happily with his mother, aunts, and cousins in their herd in Africa. Sikar ate leaves and grass. He was tall enough to reach tender leaves in the trees.

Sikar's family often traveled as far as fifty miles in a day. They walked to find food and water. Sikar loved to play games with the other elephant children. He liked to put his whole body in the water. The elephants took water in their trunks and sprayed themselves and each other. Then they used their trunks to cover themselves with dust. They didn't do it just to be dirty. The dust helped keep away insects. Sikar was as happy as a young elephant could be.

One day, his mother told him the herd was leaving, but Sikar could not go with them. He would have to stay or go off on his own. "But why, Mama?" cried Sikar. Big tears rolled down his dusty cheeks. His huge ears flapped. His wrinkled, gray face looked even more wrinkled. "I want to stay with you. I love you, Mama."

"I know, dear, but you are almost grown now. I have the other children to care for. You must go with the older males. Our herd has only females and young males. I will always love you, Sikar, but you must grow up now," Sikar's mother explained carefully.

Sikar sadly went to find the other male elephants. He saw two young males who had been in his herd last year. They looked for food together, ate, played in the water, and threw dirt on each other. They even fought a little, but only in play. It was fun not to have his mother watching and calling out to him to be careful. He was lonely at night, though.

Sikar gradually forgot his old herd. He had become a gentle giant, an African elephant who weighed six tons. One day, he passed the herd of mothers and young elephants and saw his mother. She was busy with her children, and he was busy looking for food. Sikar thought about her for a minute, but then went on his way. He enjoyed his new life, and now that he was old enough to want a family, he must find a mate of his own.

Lesson 9 Inferential Comprehension

13 From this story, you can conclude that elephants —

Ⓐ always stay with the same herd.
Ⓑ stay away from the water.
Ⓒ don't play with one another.
Ⓓ are bothered by insects.

14 Why did Sikar not want to go with the male herd?

Ⓕ He did not like those elephants.
Ⓖ He did not want to leave his mother.
Ⓗ The food they found was not as good.
Ⓙ He was bigger than the other elephants.

15 Sikar became —

Ⓐ too hungry for his first herd.
Ⓑ separated by accident from his mother.
Ⓒ an unfriendly elephant.
Ⓓ too old for his first herd.

16 The boxes show some things that happened in the story.

Sikar's mother said he should leave.		Sikar wanted a family of his own.
1	2	3

Which of these belongs in box 2?

Ⓕ Sikar was lost in the jungle.
Ⓖ Sikar joined a new herd.
Ⓗ Sikar went to live with his mother again.
Ⓙ Sikar was found in the jungle.

17 This story was written to—

Ⓐ tell about how elephants live.
Ⓑ teach a lesson about mothers and children.
Ⓒ explain how elephants find food.
Ⓓ show how large elephants are.

18 By the end of the story, Sikar was —

Ⓕ still sad about leaving his mother.
Ⓖ afraid of the larger elephants.
Ⓗ less interested in his mother.
Ⓙ unhappy with his new life.

ANSWER ROWS 13 Ⓐ Ⓑ Ⓒ Ⓓ   15 Ⓐ Ⓑ Ⓒ Ⓓ   17 Ⓐ Ⓑ Ⓒ Ⓓ
30   14 Ⓕ Ⓖ Ⓗ Ⓙ   16 Ⓕ Ⓖ Ⓗ Ⓙ   18 Ⓕ Ⓖ Ⓗ Ⓙ

Lesson 10 Test Yourself

Examples **Directions:** Read the passage. Find the best answer to each question that follows the passage.

E1

The balloon pilot turned on the burner. There was a huge whooshing sound and the balloon began to fill with hot air. Soon it started to rise into the air. In about fifteen minutes, it would be full, and they could take off.

The balloon is being filled with —

Ⓐ helium.

Ⓑ cold air.

Ⓒ hot air.

Ⓓ burning gas.

The way people entertain themselves in America has certainly changed in recent years. It was only about a hundred years ago that reading, singing, dancing, and playing musical instruments were all people had to amuse themselves. Then along came radio, and people didn't have to amuse themselves at all. They could simply listen and someone else would entertain them.

Motion pictures were the next great form of entertainment, and people could see and hear actors performing on the "big screen" in theaters around the country. The "small screen," television, soon made its way into almost every home, and people didn't even have to leave their couch to enjoy themselves. Video games and computers are the latest forms of entertainment technology, and who knows what inventions will be in our living rooms tomorrow.

1 This story is mostly about —

Ⓐ entertainers.

Ⓑ television and radio.

Ⓒ forms of entertainment.

Ⓓ technology.

2 Which of these came first?

Ⓕ Computers

Ⓖ Motion pictures

Ⓗ Television

Ⓙ Radio

For Number 3, choose the best answer to the question.

3 The giant picked up the two children and said, "Gosh, you've been so nice to me. What can I do to thank you?"

This sentence would most likely be found in a —

Ⓐ fairy tale.

Ⓑ biography.

Ⓒ newspaper article.

Ⓓ mystery story.

GO

ANSWER ROW E1 Ⓐ Ⓑ Ⓒ Ⓓ   1 Ⓐ Ⓑ Ⓒ Ⓓ   2 Ⓕ Ⓖ Ⓗ Ⓙ   3 Ⓐ Ⓑ Ⓒ Ⓓ

How did Lilia feel about visiting her grandmother?

Lilia tried hard to keep the tears from filling her large, brown eyes. She felt like a heavy lump was in her chest. School was out, and all her friends were happily planning swimming lessons and family vacations. Lilia's mother had just told her she would have to go far away to spend the summer at Grandmother's. Lilia loved Grandmother, but she would be lonely without her family and friends in the neighborhood.

Lilia's mother put her arms around Lilia and brushed back her long, dark hair. Mrs. McGill had been sick and needed a great deal of rest this summer. Grandmother would take good care of Lilia, and she would come home at the end of summer. Everything would be better then. Lilia sniffed and nodded. She knew her mother was right, but she was still sad.

On the day she arrived, Lilia tried to find something wrong at Grandmother's house, but she couldn't. It had flowers, trees, and a white fence. Grandmother baked bread and cooked the same kind of food that Lilia's mother made at home. Grandmother smiled and told her, "I'm so glad you've come, Lilia."

Grandmother showed Lilia her pet bird, Bitsy, and the dog, Charley. Bitsy chirped at her, and Charley brought his ball for Lilia to throw.

That afternoon, Lilia saw some children next door. She asked Grandmother about them. Grandmother said, "Oh, that's Sally and her brother, Sid. They are twins, and they are the same age as you. I know you'll get along and play together. Their mother and I have lots of things planned for the three of you."

Lilia smiled. She would miss her family and friends back home, but this might be a good summer after all!

4 In the story, Lilia felt—

- Ⓕ sad and then happy.
- Ⓖ sad all through the story.
- Ⓗ happy and then disappointed.
- Ⓙ happy all through the story.

5 This story is written to show—

- Ⓐ children have a hard time when their parents are sick.
- Ⓑ things often work out better than you think at first.
- Ⓒ a child can never be happy away from home for the summer.
- Ⓓ grandmothers are not as much fun as mothers.

6 Lilia's grandmother had—

- Ⓕ no children as neighbors.
- Ⓖ a small house with no yard.
- Ⓗ a swimming pool in her back yard.
- Ⓙ a bird and a dog for pets.

7 Lilia was a girl who—

- Ⓐ tried not to show her mother that she was sad.
- Ⓑ did not get along with other children her own age.
- Ⓒ was rude to her grandmother when she went to visit.
- Ⓓ complained because she was unhappy going to her grandmother's.

8 Why did Lilia smile in the last paragraph?

- Ⓕ She knew she would be spending the summer at her own home.
- Ⓖ She didn't want Grandmother to see her cry.
- Ⓗ She knew she would be happy being away from home.
- Ⓙ She loved animals, and Grandmother had two pets.

9 Which words in the story show that Grandmother was trying to make things fun for Lilia?

- Ⓐ ...Lilia saw some children next door...
- Ⓑ She would miss her family and friends back home...
- Ⓒ Their mother and I have lots of things planned...
- Ⓓ ... this might be a good summer...

10 Which would be a good title for this story?

- Ⓕ My Grandmother
- Ⓖ A Surprising Summer
- Ⓗ New Friends
- Ⓙ Bitsy and Charley

Lucy sat very still as the plane took off. She liked flying, but always felt a little funny when the plane took off and landed. This plane was smaller than any other she had ever been on, and she didn't know what it would be like.

The take-off was smooth, and in a few minutes, they were flying high above the ground. All around them, Lucy could see the ocean.

The plane headed south from Miami toward Key West. Lucy, her mother, and her two brothers were going there to visit her father. He was in the Coast Guard and was stationed in Key West.

Lucy looked out the window and saw a chain of islands. Her mother said they were the Florida Keys. A road and a series of bridges connected the islands. Key West was the last island in the chain.

"Mom, how come they are called keys?"

"It's from the Spanish word *cayo*, which means island or reef. The first European explorers here were from Spain."

The water below had lots of different colors. The deepest water was dark blue, and along the shore, it was very light. In between, there were many shades of blue. On this background of blue were lots of boats, some with sails and some with motors. As the boats moved across the surface, they left streaks of white in their wake.

Lucy heard the sound of the engines change and the plane started its descent. In a few minutes, she would see her father for the first time in weeks. It would also be the beginning of a vacation she would remember forever.

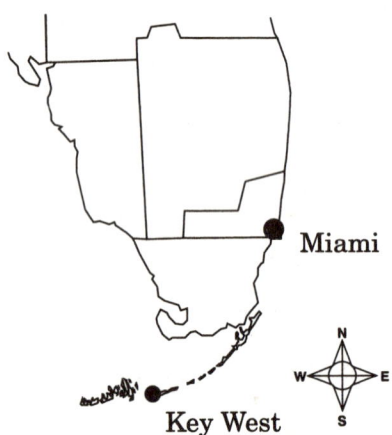

Lesson 10 Test Yourself

11 Which of these is true about Lucy?

- Ⓐ She had never flown on a plane before.
- Ⓑ She was afraid of flying.
- Ⓒ She often flies on small planes.
- Ⓓ She had never flown on a plane this small before.

12 When Lucy flies back to Miami, in which direction will she travel?

- Ⓕ North
- Ⓖ South
- Ⓗ East
- Ⓙ West

13 How did Lucy first know the plane was about to land?

- Ⓐ She saw the airport.
- Ⓑ The pilot turned the plane toward the airport.
- Ⓒ The sound of the engines changed.
- Ⓓ The pilot made an announcement over the intercom.

14 What can you conclude about the water around the Florida Keys?

- Ⓕ Deeper water is lighter in color than shallow water.
- Ⓖ Deeper water is darker in color than shallow water.
- Ⓗ It seems to be very rough.
- Ⓙ It seems to be very calm.

15 Why was Lucy going to Key West?

- Ⓐ To visit her father
- Ⓑ To visit her mother
- Ⓒ To move there
- Ⓓ To go to school there

16 What kinds of things do you think Lucy will do in Key West?

- Ⓕ Climb mountains, ski, and go ice skating
- Ⓖ Stay inside and watch television because it is cold
- Ⓗ Swim, ride in a boat, and lie on the beach
- Ⓙ Visit farms and ride on a tractor

35

ANSWER ROWS 11 Ⓐ Ⓑ Ⓒ Ⓓ   13 Ⓐ Ⓑ Ⓒ Ⓓ   15 Ⓐ Ⓑ Ⓒ Ⓓ
             12 Ⓕ Ⓖ Ⓗ Ⓙ   14 Ⓕ Ⓖ Ⓗ Ⓙ   16 Ⓕ Ⓖ Ⓗ Ⓙ

NUMBER RIGHT _____

Name and Answer Sheet

To the Student:

These tests will give you a chance to put the tips you have learned to work.

A few last reminders…

- Be sure you understand all the directions before you begin each test. You may ask the teacher questions about the directions if you do not understand them.
- Work as quickly as you can during each test.
- When you change an answer, be sure to erase your first mark completely.
- You can guess at an answer or skip difficult items and go back to them later.
- Use the tips you have learned whenever you can.
- It is OK to be a little nervous. You may even do better.

Now that you have completed the lessons in this unit, you are on your way to scoring high!

Name and Answer Sheet

PART 1 VOCABULARY

E1 Ⓐ Ⓑ Ⓒ Ⓓ	4 Ⓕ Ⓖ Ⓗ Ⓙ	10 Ⓕ Ⓖ Ⓗ Ⓙ	16 Ⓕ Ⓖ Ⓗ Ⓙ	21 Ⓐ Ⓑ Ⓒ Ⓓ	25 Ⓐ Ⓑ Ⓒ Ⓓ
E2 Ⓕ Ⓖ Ⓗ Ⓙ	5 Ⓐ Ⓑ Ⓒ Ⓓ	11 Ⓐ Ⓑ Ⓒ Ⓓ	17 Ⓐ Ⓑ Ⓒ Ⓓ	22 Ⓕ Ⓖ Ⓗ Ⓙ	26 Ⓕ Ⓖ Ⓗ Ⓙ
E3 Ⓐ Ⓑ Ⓒ Ⓓ	6 Ⓕ Ⓖ Ⓗ Ⓙ	12 Ⓕ Ⓖ Ⓗ Ⓙ	18 Ⓕ Ⓖ Ⓗ Ⓙ	23 Ⓐ Ⓑ Ⓒ Ⓓ	27 Ⓐ Ⓑ Ⓒ Ⓓ
1 Ⓐ Ⓑ Ⓒ Ⓓ	7 Ⓐ Ⓑ Ⓒ Ⓓ	13 Ⓐ Ⓑ Ⓒ Ⓓ	19 Ⓐ Ⓑ Ⓒ Ⓓ	24 Ⓕ Ⓖ Ⓗ Ⓙ	28 Ⓕ Ⓖ Ⓗ Ⓙ
2 Ⓕ Ⓖ Ⓗ Ⓙ	8 Ⓕ Ⓖ Ⓗ Ⓙ	14 Ⓕ Ⓖ Ⓗ Ⓙ	20 Ⓕ Ⓖ Ⓗ Ⓙ		
3 Ⓐ Ⓑ Ⓒ Ⓓ	9 Ⓐ Ⓑ Ⓒ Ⓓ	15 Ⓐ Ⓑ Ⓒ Ⓓ			

PART 2 READING COMPREHENSION

E1 Ⓐ Ⓑ Ⓒ Ⓓ	5 Ⓐ Ⓑ Ⓒ Ⓓ	10 Ⓕ Ⓖ Ⓗ Ⓙ	15 Ⓐ Ⓑ Ⓒ Ⓓ	19 Ⓐ Ⓑ Ⓒ Ⓓ	22 Ⓕ Ⓖ Ⓗ Ⓙ
1 Ⓐ Ⓑ Ⓒ Ⓓ	6 Ⓕ Ⓖ Ⓗ Ⓙ	11 Ⓐ Ⓑ Ⓒ Ⓓ	16 Ⓕ Ⓖ Ⓗ Ⓙ	20 Ⓕ Ⓖ Ⓗ Ⓙ	23 Ⓐ Ⓑ Ⓒ Ⓓ
2 Ⓕ Ⓖ Ⓗ Ⓙ	7 Ⓐ Ⓑ Ⓒ Ⓓ	12 Ⓕ Ⓖ Ⓗ Ⓙ	17 Ⓐ Ⓑ Ⓒ Ⓓ	21 Ⓐ Ⓑ Ⓒ Ⓓ	24 Ⓕ Ⓖ Ⓗ Ⓙ
3 Ⓐ Ⓑ Ⓒ Ⓓ	8 Ⓕ Ⓖ Ⓗ Ⓙ	13 Ⓐ Ⓑ Ⓒ Ⓓ	18 Ⓕ Ⓖ Ⓗ Ⓙ		
4 Ⓕ Ⓖ Ⓗ Ⓙ	9 Ⓐ Ⓑ Ⓒ Ⓓ	14 Ⓕ Ⓖ Ⓗ Ⓙ			

Test Practice

Part 1 Vocabulary

Examples **Directions:** For items E1 and 1-9, read the phrase with the underlined word. Find the word that means the same or almost the same. For item E2, mark the answer that is the opposite of the underlined word. For item E3, find the word that best fits in both sentences.

E1 a <u>huge</u> rock

- Ⓐ heavy
- Ⓑ long
- Ⓒ large
- Ⓓ small

E2 <u>borrow</u> a pen

- Ⓕ steal
- Ⓖ lend
- Ⓗ lose
- Ⓙ find

E3 Do you _____ oranges?
Jim has a bicycle just _____ mine.

- Ⓐ enjoy
- Ⓑ about
- Ⓒ squeeze
- Ⓓ like

1 <u>nasty</u> weather

- Ⓐ bad
- Ⓑ pleasant
- Ⓒ normal
- Ⓓ acceptable

2 give <u>commands</u>

- Ⓕ presents
- Ⓖ statements
- Ⓗ changes
- Ⓙ orders

3 <u>stay</u> home

- Ⓐ allow
- Ⓑ remain
- Ⓒ respond
- Ⓓ leave

4 Her business is <u>reliable</u>.

- Ⓕ dependable
- Ⓖ successful
- Ⓗ crowded
- Ⓙ new

5 Are you <u>certain</u> about that?

- Ⓐ happy
- Ⓑ unsure
- Ⓒ sure
- Ⓓ sad

6 a <u>cautious</u> person

- Ⓕ annoying
- Ⓖ friendly
- Ⓗ careful
- Ⓙ healthy

7 to <u>display</u> a picture

- Ⓐ paint
- Ⓑ show
- Ⓒ buy
- Ⓓ sell

8 To be <u>frail</u> is to be —

- Ⓕ weak
- Ⓖ strong
- Ⓗ lost
- Ⓙ confused

9 To <u>discard</u> is to —

- Ⓐ find
- Ⓑ trip over
- Ⓒ lose
- Ⓓ throw away

Part 1 Vocabulary

Directions: For items 10-14, read the phrase with the underlined word. Find the word that means the opposite of the underlined word.

10 That trail might be <u>dangerous</u>.

- Ⓕ expensive
- Ⓖ enjoyable
- Ⓗ foolish
- Ⓙ safe

11 The group stayed <u>together</u> at the zoo.

- Ⓐ close
- Ⓑ far away
- Ⓒ apart
- Ⓓ with one another

12 The story about the family of bears made Ted <u>smile</u>.

- Ⓕ frown
- Ⓖ grin
- Ⓗ feel good
- Ⓙ feel amused

13 a cool <u>evening</u>

- Ⓐ drink
- Ⓑ friend
- Ⓒ morning
- Ⓓ product

14 <u>allow</u> a visit

- Ⓕ permit
- Ⓖ make
- Ⓗ conduct
- Ⓙ forbid

Directions: For numbers 15-16, find the word that fits in both sentences. For numbers 17-18, find the answer in which the underlined word is used the same as in the sentence in the box.

15 The swim _____ took place on Saturday morning at nine.

Where did you _____ Sandra?

- Ⓐ meet
- Ⓑ find
- Ⓒ see
- Ⓓ match

16 Can you _____ in the ocean?

Our _____ led the parade.

- Ⓕ swim
- Ⓖ band
- Ⓗ dive
- Ⓙ float

17 My <u>back</u> was sore after the game.

In which sentence does the word <u>back</u> mean the same thing as in the sentence above?

- Ⓐ Come <u>back</u> when you have finished.
- Ⓑ The dog is in <u>back</u> of the house.
- Ⓒ The pack on her <u>back</u> was heavy.
- Ⓓ The light in the <u>back</u> room is on.

18 How much did that <u>stamp</u> cost?

In which sentence does the word <u>stamp</u> mean the same thing as in the sentence above?

- Ⓕ <u>Stamp</u> your name on this form.
- Ⓖ This machine can <u>stamp</u> metal.
- Ⓗ A horse will often <u>stamp</u> its feet.
- Ⓙ There's no <u>stamp</u> on the envelope.

Part 1 Vocabulary

Directions: Read the sentences with the blanks. Choose the answer that fits best in the sentence or means the same as the underlined word.

19 We can all _____ the hall.
Find the word that means to make the hall beautiful.

Ⓐ visit
Ⓒ decorate
Ⓑ replace
Ⓓ attend

20 That light is too _____ for reading.
Which word means the light wasn't very bright?

Ⓕ dim
Ⓗ harsh
Ⓖ high
Ⓙ shallow

21 The picnic will have to be delayed.
Delayed means —

Ⓐ started
Ⓒ planned
Ⓑ postponed
Ⓓ enjoyed

22 Did Brenda reply to your question?
Reply means —

Ⓕ accept
Ⓗ startle
Ⓖ harness
Ⓙ answer

The dinner you served was __(23)__. We are grateful you remembered us. We'll __(24)__ you to our house soon.

23 Ⓐ extended
Ⓒ delicious
Ⓑ realized
Ⓓ famous

24 Ⓕ invite
Ⓗ enjoy
Ⓖ accept
Ⓙ frequent

The manager was __(25)__ with what the workers did. They finished on time and also saved a great deal of money for the __(26)__.

25 Ⓐ disappointed
Ⓒ busy
Ⓑ happy
Ⓓ confusing

26 Ⓕ company
Ⓗ reasons
Ⓖ benefit
Ⓙ acceptance

Be sure to __(27)__ Clark Street. There's been an accident and traffic is __(28)__ than usual.

27 Ⓐ travel
Ⓒ wait
Ⓑ standard
Ⓓ avoid

28 Ⓕ almost
Ⓗ moving
Ⓖ heavier
Ⓙ nearby

Part 2 Reading Comprehension

Directions: Read each passage, then answer each question. You can look back to the passage to answer the questions.

E1

The cat was curled up in a tiny ball beside the fire. When she heard Martin walk into the room, she opened one eye first and then the other. Domino slowly stood up and stretched. She blinked twice and followed him toward the kitchen.

The cat was probably —

Ⓐ playing.
Ⓑ hunting.
Ⓒ purring.
Ⓓ sleeping.

The travelers found themselves in a forest of talking trees. Just then, all the trees began talking at once. They were so loud that it was impossible to understand what they were saying.

1 Which sentence is most likely to come next in the story?

Ⓐ Once upon a time a group of travelers started on a long journey.

Ⓑ No one knew where they were and they became frightened.

Ⓒ Suddenly, the biggest tree said, "Quiet, everyone!"

Ⓓ The outside of the trunk of a tree is called the bark.

What I remember most about that big old house in Iowa was the kitchen, a room that was always warm and always smelled wonderful.

2 This sentence would most likely be found in —

Ⓕ a newspaper article.
Ⓖ an autobiography.
Ⓗ a fairy tale.
Ⓙ a science book.

3 Which of these would most likely be found in a newspaper article?

Ⓐ "Now hold on there," said the sheriff, "we don't put up with things like that in this town."

Ⓑ It wasn't a star they were looking at, but a spaceship, and it was coming right at them.

Ⓒ Guido said good-bye to his family, picked up his bags, and joined the crowd walking toward the ship.

Ⓓ A recent report from the school board stated that there are more students in school than ever before.

4 Sally is reading a book called *Home Gardening for Young People*. Which of these sentences would most likely be at the beginning of the book?

Ⓕ After you have planted the seeds, you'll have to keep them watered so they don't dry out.

Ⓖ Few things are as rewarding as tending a garden.

Ⓗ Now comes the fun part, eating the vegetables you have raised.

Ⓙ The most difficult part of having a garden is making sure that weeds don't take over.

Last Sunday, my dog Buddy started scratching his face. Pretty soon, it was red and sore. I was really worried.

"Mom, something is wrong with Buddy. Look at his face."

"This doesn't look very good, Lucas. Let's put some medicine on it and see what happens. If it doesn't get any better, we'll have to take him to the doctor."

I rubbed the medicine on Buddy's face and was very careful not to get it into his eyes. He didn't like it very much, but he held still for me.

The next day, he was even worse, so Dad stayed home from work, and he and I took Buddy to the veterinarian. The doctor examined Buddy and gave us some pills. We had to give them to Buddy three times a day. The doctor said it would be easiest if we mixed it into food or a treat. The doctor also gave us a special collar that would keep Buddy from scratching his face. When we put the collar on, Buddy looked like a clown, but I felt bad for him.

I gave Buddy his medicine every day just like the doctor said. For a day or two it didn't seem to help. Then Buddy stopped trying to scratch his face. Pretty soon, his face started to get better.

A week later, my Aunt Janelle and I took Buddy back to the doctor. He examined Buddy again and said he was okay. The veterinarian thought that Buddy had an allergy, kind of like when I start to sneeze when Dad cuts the lawn. He said we should keep an eye on Buddy to see if we could find out what he was allergic to. If we found out, we could avoid it in the future.

5   How do you think Lucas felt at the end of the story?

   Ⓐ Worried because Buddy had an allergy

   Ⓑ Happy because Buddy had an allergy

   Ⓒ Disappointed because the doctor couldn't fix the problem

   Ⓓ Relieved because Buddy was getting better

6   Who is telling this story?

   Ⓕ Lucas

   Ⓖ Buddy

   Ⓗ Aunt Janelle

   Ⓙ The doctor

7   What made Buddy look like a clown?

   Ⓐ Scratches on his nose

   Ⓑ The medicine on his face

   Ⓒ A special collar

   Ⓓ The pills

8   We know that Lucas is a responsible person because he —

   Ⓕ rode in the car to the doctor with Aunt Janelle.

   Ⓖ gave Buddy his medicine every day.

   Ⓗ tried to get to school on time.

   Ⓙ felt bad because Lucas had to wear a funny collar.

9   A lesson you can learn from this story is to —

   Ⓐ avoid cutting the grass when the wind is blowing.

   Ⓑ keep dogs inside as much as possible.

   Ⓒ avoid things to which you are allergic.

   Ⓓ be careful when you put a new collar on a dog or cat.

He Changed the World

"Chris. Christopher. Chris-to-pher! Come home for dinner!" Chris heard his mother's voice, and walked home slowly. He was watching a ship in the harbor near his home. The sailors were unloading wonderful things that had been brought from far away. There were mysterious bundles and smells that Chris did not recognize. The ship had just come from Asia. The sailors were sunburned and happy. They talked to the young boy on the dock.

When he reached his home, Christopher told his mother, "A ship just came in. It was wonderful. When I grow up, I want to be a sailor. I want to go places and see things."

The boy was Christopher Columbus. He lived in Genoa, Italy, a city by the sea. Genoa was one of the busiest seaports in the world when Chris was born in 1451. He did become a sailor when he was a teenager, and he did see the world.

In the 1400s, ships carried things from Asia to Italy and other places. They brought jewels, ivory, silks, and spices. The ships carried the goods part of the way, and then they had to be unloaded so camels and other animals could carry everything across land. Then the goods would be loaded on another ship to finish the trip.

Christopher Columbus thought he could find a way to go all the way to Asia by water. Many people in his time thought the earth was flat, but he thought it was round. He wanted to sail west to reach Asia. If Columbus could find a new, shorter route to Asia, he would become rich and famous.

Columbus was not poor, but he did not have the money to buy ships for such a trip. He couldn't find any money in his own country. He went to the king and queen of Spain, Ferdinand and Isabella. They first said no, but they changed their minds. They agreed to buy Columbus three ships and give him money to make his trip.

After being at sea for two difficult months and facing many dangers, Columbus saw land. He and his sailors thought they had arrived in Asia and were very excited. They had not found Asia, however. Instead, they had reached the New World, what we now call America. Columbus never got rich, but many others followed. He had changed the world forever.

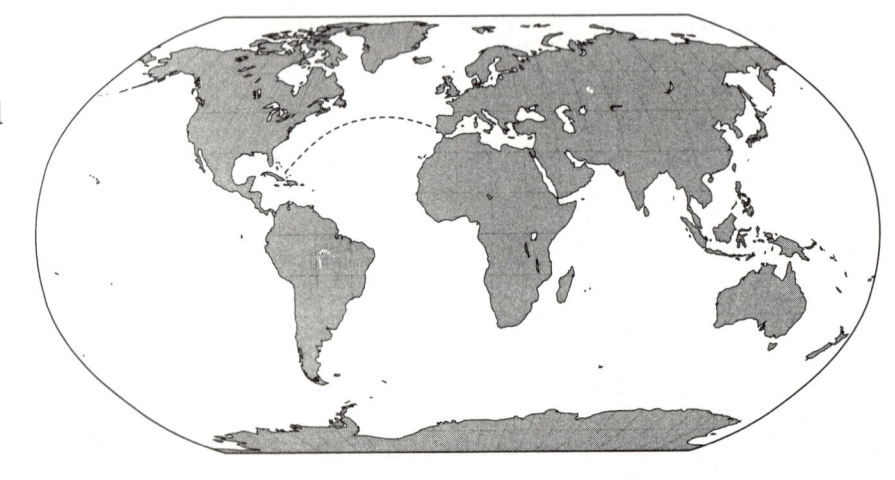

10 Why didn't Christopher Columbus sail in his own ships?

- Ⓕ The king would not let him.
- Ⓖ He couldn't find any sailors for his ships.
- Ⓗ Only kings and queens could own ships.
- Ⓙ He didn't have enough money.

11 This story was written to tell the reader—

- Ⓐ how Columbus spent his fortune.
- Ⓑ about sailing ships in the 1400s.
- Ⓒ about ships going to Asia.
- Ⓓ how Columbus achieved his dream.

12 What word in the story means "difficult to explain, strange, unusual"?

- Ⓕ Mysterious
- Ⓖ Recognize
- Ⓗ Explorer
- Ⓙ Seaport

13 Christopher became interested in sailing because —

- Ⓐ his father was a sailor.
- Ⓑ he dreamed about an adventure.
- Ⓒ he lived by the sea.
- Ⓓ his family owned ships.

14 What mistake did Christopher Columbus and his sailors make?

- Ⓕ They sailed in a circle and landed in Europe.
- Ⓖ They found Asia instead of America.
- Ⓗ They found America instead of Asia.
- Ⓙ They had not really found land.

15 Which of these does this story lead you to believe?

- Ⓐ Columbus did not know about Asia when he left Spain.
- Ⓑ Columbus did not know about the New World when he left Spain.
- Ⓒ The king and queen made Columbus a rich man.
- Ⓓ Columbus knew the world was flat but tried anyway.

16 Which of these is most like what happened in the story?

- Ⓕ Bridgette was looking for her homework and found a ring she had lost a week ago.
- Ⓖ Andrew enjoys sailing and hopes to own a boat when he grows up.
- Ⓗ Kate and her family planned a vacation carefully and really enjoyed their trip to a national park.
- Ⓙ Jake surprised his sister by giving her a party on her birthday.

Schedule for Camp Tonawanabee

Week of July 8 - 13

Eight and nine-year-old campers should check in at camp office between 12 noon and 5 P.M., July 7.

7:00 - 8:30	Wake up, breakfast, clean up	1:30 - 2:30	Ping-pong for 8-year-olds
8:30 - 9:30	Boys' swimming		Crafts for 9-year-olds
	Girls' basketball	2:30 - 3:00	Break
9:30 - 10:00	Break	3:00 - 4:00	Horseshoes
10:00 - 11:00	Boys' basketball	4:00 - 5:00	Hiking
	Girls' swimming	5:00 - 6:30	Dinner, rest
11:00 - 12:30	Lunch, rest	6:30 - 7:30	Softball or volleyball
12:30 - 1:30	Crafts for 8-year-olds	7:30 - 8:30	Movie or group singing
	Ping-pong for 9-year-olds	8:30 - 9:00	Cabin meetings, snacks
		9:00 - 9:30	Ready for bed, lights out

For more information, call Marissa Johnson at 903-555-1214.

Counselors for 8-year-olds:
Adam Sands, head counselor, boys; Jack Smithey; Charlie Carlson.
Mary Jones, head counselor, girls; Sue Martin; Ericka Stevens

Counselors for 9-year-olds:
Joe Johnson, head counselor, boys; Cedric White; Aaron Lang.
Lisa Gomez, head counselor, girls; Heather Case; Shalonda Moore

Part 2   Reading Comprehension

17 At what time do the boys have swimming?

- Ⓐ 8:00 - 9:00
- Ⓑ 8:30 - 9:30
- Ⓒ 10:00 - 11:00
- Ⓓ 1:30 - 2:30

18 Which of these activities is <u>not</u> in the morning?

- Ⓕ Swimming
- Ⓖ Crafts
- Ⓗ Breakfast
- Ⓙ Basketball

19 Sylvester is a 9-year-old boy. He started a braided leather key chain in crafts class on Tuesday. At what time on Wednesday will he go to crafts again to finish it?

- Ⓐ 11:30 - 12:30
- Ⓑ 12:30 - 1:30
- Ⓒ 1:30 - 2:30
- Ⓓ 3:00 - 4:00

20 What are the rest times for all campers?

- Ⓕ After lunch and after dinner
- Ⓖ Before lunch and after dinner
- Ⓗ Before lunch and before dinner
- Ⓙ After lunch and before dinner

21 Whom would you call for more information about the camp?

- Ⓐ Marissa Johnson
- Ⓑ Joe Johnson
- Ⓒ Mary Jones
- Ⓓ Charlie Carlson

22 Eight-year-old Toby and 9-year-old Tina are a brother and sister going to Camp Tonawanabee this summer. Which activity will they have together?

- Ⓕ Crafts
- Ⓖ Ping-pong
- Ⓗ Hiking
- Ⓙ Swimming

23 Who is the head counselor for 9-year-old girls?

- Ⓐ Joe Johnson
- Ⓑ Mary Jones
- Ⓒ Sue Martin
- Ⓓ Lisa Gomez

24 Which of these happens last?

- Ⓕ Basketball
- Ⓖ Boy's swimming
- Ⓗ Ping-pong
- Ⓙ Softball

Table of Contents
Language

Unit 1   **Language Mechanics**

Lesson		Page
❏ 1	Capitalization	49
❏ 2	Punctuation	50
❏ 3	Capitalization and Punctuation	51
❏ 4	Test Yourself	53

Unit 2   **Language Expression**

Lesson		Page
❏ 5	Nouns and Pronouns	56
❏ 6	Verbs	58
❏ 7	Adjectives	59
❏ 8	Sentences	60
❏ 9	Paragraphs	63
❏ 10	Test Yourself	66

Unit 3   **Spelling**

Lesson		Page
❏ 11	Spelling Skills	72
❏ 12	Test Yourself	74

Unit 4   **Study Skills**

Lesson		Page
❏ 13	Study Skills	76
❏ 14	Test Yourself	79
❏	Name and Answer Sheet	81

Unit 5   **Test Practice**

Part		Page
❏ 1	Language Mechanics	83
❏ 2	Language Expression	86
❏ 3	Spelling	90
❏ 4	Study Skills	92

UNIT 1 LANGUAGE MECHANICS
Lesson 1 Capitalization

Examples **Directions:** For items A and 1-3, mark the answer that shows a capital letter missing. For items B and 4-5, mark the answer that shows the correct capitalization.

A	School	will start	in september.	None
	Ⓐ	Ⓑ	Ⓒ	Ⓓ

B   That dress was worn by _____ .
- Ⓕ Queen elizabeth
- Ⓖ Queen Elizabeth
- Ⓗ queen Elizabeth
- Ⓙ queen elizabeth

Tips

Sentences and proper nouns begin with capital letters.

If no capital letters are missing, mark the space for "None."

Practice

1	she went	to the beach	last week.	None
	Ⓐ	Ⓑ	Ⓒ	Ⓓ

2	The name	of the book	is A Terrible Storm.	None
	Ⓕ	Ⓖ	Ⓗ	Ⓙ

3	Which part	of france	did you like best?	None
	Ⓐ	Ⓑ	Ⓒ	Ⓓ

4   My _____ came to visit during the holiday.
- Ⓕ Best friend
- Ⓖ best Friend
- Ⓗ Best Friend
- Ⓙ best friend

5   Did you walk to school on _____ ?
- Ⓐ Friday morning
- Ⓑ friday morning
- Ⓒ friday Morning
- Ⓓ Friday Morning

GO

ANSWER ROWS A Ⓐ Ⓑ Ⓒ Ⓓ   1 Ⓐ Ⓑ Ⓒ Ⓓ   3 Ⓐ Ⓑ Ⓒ Ⓓ   5 Ⓐ Ⓑ Ⓒ Ⓓ
             B Ⓕ Ⓖ Ⓗ Ⓙ   2 Ⓕ Ⓖ Ⓗ Ⓙ   4 Ⓕ Ⓖ Ⓗ Ⓙ

Lesson 2   Punctuation

Examples   **Directions:** For items A and 1-3, mark the answer that shows the correct punctuation. For item 4, mark the correct answer. For items B and 5, mark the answer that shows where the punctuation is missing.

A   Who said it was going to rain today?

Ⓐ .   Ⓑ ,   Ⓒ !   Ⓓ None

B   Ⓕ   The gray cat watched
    Ⓖ   the birds outside Her
    Ⓗ   tail curled back and forth.
    Ⓙ   (No mistakes)

Tips   First look for missing punctuation at the end of the sentence. Then look for missing punctuation inside the sentence.

If the punctuation is correct, mark the space for "None" or "No mistakes."

Practice

1   The books are on the shelf

Ⓐ .   Ⓑ ,   Ⓒ ?   Ⓓ None

2   Where did you put the bag of groceries?

Ⓕ .   Ⓖ ,   Ⓗ !   Ⓙ None

3   Close the door quickly or the cat will get out

Ⓐ .   Ⓑ !   Ⓒ ?   Ⓓ None

4   The pizza _____ ready so we had to wait for a while.

   Ⓕ   wasn't
   Ⓖ   wasnt
   Ⓗ   wasnt'
   Ⓙ   was'nt

5   Ⓐ   The gardener planted
    Ⓑ   tulips roses and daisies
    Ⓒ   along the sidewalk.
    Ⓓ   (No mistakes)

Lesson 3   Capitalization and Punctuation

Examples   **Directions:** Mark the answer that shows the correct capitalization and punctuation. Mark the space "Correct as it is" if the underlined part is correct.

A
- Ⓐ Which coat is yours?
- Ⓑ Mine is the red one
- Ⓒ where did you buy it?
- Ⓓ Hang your coat in the closet?

(B) Winning the race <u>won't</u> be easy.

B
- Ⓕ Won't
- Ⓖ wont'
- Ⓗ Wont'
- Ⓙ Correct as it is

Tips   First think about capitalization errors in the sentence. Then think about punctuation errors.

Remember, choose the answer that is correct.

Practice

1
- Ⓐ Which State is the largest?
- Ⓑ South carolina has great beaches.
- Ⓒ My grandmother spent the night in Chicago Illinois.
- Ⓓ The driver knew she was a few hours from Houston, Texas.

2
- Ⓕ we can all meet at the park.
- Ⓖ Teresa said her brothers want to play with us
- Ⓗ Did you remember the basketball?
- Ⓙ Randy will be a little late?

---

(3)   <u>August 10, 1994</u>

Dear Irma,
    The lake is warm enough for swimming. I hope you will come up soon for a visit.

(4)   <u>Your Friend</u>
        Enrique

3
- Ⓐ August 10 1994
- Ⓑ August, 10, 1994
- Ⓒ august 10, 1994
- Ⓓ Correct as it is

4
- Ⓕ Your friend,
- Ⓖ Your Friend,
- Ⓗ your friend,
- Ⓙ Correct as it is

GO

Lesson 3   Capitalization and Punctuation

5 The _____ tail started to wag when we walked into the room.

- Ⓐ puppys
- Ⓑ puppy's
- Ⓒ puppies
- Ⓓ puppie's

6 A _____ usually has many traffic problems.

- Ⓕ Large City
- Ⓖ large City
- Ⓗ Large city
- Ⓙ large city

Read this diary entry and answer questions 7–10. The diary has groups of underlined words. The questions will ask about them.

<u>Uncle richard</u> did the strangest thing today. He built something that looked
(1)   (2)
like a bird house and said it was for bats. He is going to put it on the side of
                                                           (3)
the house near the roof. I never heard of anything called a <u>bat house?</u> My
                                                             (4)   (5)
uncle explained that bats are harmless to people but eat lots of insects like

<u>mosquitoes flies, and moths</u>. If the bat house works, <u>we'll be able</u> to sit on
                                                          (6)
the deck and not be bothered by bugs.

7 In sentence 1, <u>Uncle richard</u> is best written—

- Ⓐ uncle richard
- Ⓑ Uncle richard
- Ⓒ Uncle Richard
- Ⓓ as it is

8 In sentence 4, <u>bat house?</u> is best written—

- Ⓕ bat house.
- Ⓖ bat house
- Ⓗ bat house,
- Ⓙ as it is

9 In sentence 5, <u>mosquitoes flies, and moths</u> is best written—

- Ⓐ mosquitoes, flies, and moths
- Ⓑ mosquitoes flies and moths
- Ⓒ mosquitoes, flies, and, moths
- Ⓓ as it is

10 In sentence 6, <u>we'll be able</u> is best written—

- Ⓕ well be able
- Ⓖ well' be able
- Ⓗ wel'l be able
- Ⓙ as it is

Lesson 4 Test Yourself

Examples **Directions:** Mark the answer that shows incorrect capitalization or punctuation. Mark the space "None" if there are no errors.

E1
the table	in the kitchen	is too small.	None
Ⓐ	Ⓑ	Ⓒ	Ⓓ

E2
- Ⓕ Arizona became a state
- Ⓖ on February 14 1912.
- Ⓗ Its capital is Phoenix.
- Ⓙ *(No mistakes)*

1
The next book	I plan to read	is A dog named Ollie.	None
Ⓐ	Ⓑ	Ⓒ	Ⓓ

2
My friends	are going bowling	on thursday night.	None
Ⓕ	Ⓖ	Ⓗ	Ⓙ

3
how many	pieces of bread	did you eat?	None
Ⓐ	Ⓑ	Ⓒ	Ⓓ

---

4 The bus arrived at _____ more than three hours late.
- Ⓕ the Station
- Ⓖ The station
- Ⓗ The Station
- Ⓙ the station

5 Can you tell me how to get to _____ ?
- Ⓐ Baker street
- Ⓑ Baker Street
- Ⓒ baker street
- Ⓓ baker Street

---

6 Lots of squirrels live in the park.

　Ⓕ ,　　Ⓖ !　　Ⓗ ?　　Ⓙ None

7 Don't touch that plant

　Ⓐ .　　Ⓑ !　　Ⓒ ?　　Ⓓ None

8 Haven't we been here before

　Ⓕ .　　Ⓖ !　　Ⓗ ?　　Ⓙ None

GO

Lesson 4 Test Yourself

Directions: For items 9-12, mark the answer that shows the correct capitalization and punctuation. For items 13-14, mark the space that shows the part of the sentence that has incorrect punctuation. Mark the space "No mistakes" if there are no errors.

9 Our coach _____ told us who the captain will be.

- Ⓐ hasnt
- Ⓑ hasnt'
- Ⓒ has'nt
- Ⓓ hasn't

10 What is the correct abbreviation for the word Monday?

- Ⓕ Mon
- Ⓖ Mon.
- Ⓗ Mon,
- Ⓙ Mon;

11 Ⓐ Will you go to the park with us.

Ⓑ I drew a picture of the ducks on the pond in the park.

Ⓒ Many ducks and other birds fly south for the Winter.

Ⓓ The park is on central avenue.

12 Ⓕ Is that Carol's house?

Ⓖ Don't forget, to call home if you are going to be late.

Ⓗ Who wi'll carry the bags?

Ⓙ Both of them, can go with us.

13 Ⓐ We helped Mr Phillips
Ⓑ fix his car. It had
Ⓒ a flat tire this morning.
Ⓓ *(No mistakes)*

14 Ⓕ The box we received had
Ⓖ gifts from my grandmother for
Ⓗ my mother my father and me.
Ⓙ *(No mistakes)*

Directions: For items 15-16, read the letter. Mark the answer that shows the correct punctuation for the underlined phrases. Mark the space "Correct as it is" if there are no errors.

(15)   March 5, 1994

Dear Pete,

Thanks for the shirt. All the kids at school wish they had one. They
(16)   think Montana is a neat place I hope we can visit you soon.

Your cousin,

Susan

15 Ⓐ March 5 1994

Ⓑ March 5 1994,

Ⓒ March, 5 1994

Ⓓ Correct as it is

16 Ⓕ place, I hope

Ⓖ place I hope.

Ⓗ place. I hope

Ⓙ Correct as it is

GO

ANSWER ROWS 9 Ⓐ Ⓑ Ⓒ Ⓓ 11 Ⓐ Ⓑ Ⓒ Ⓓ 13 Ⓐ Ⓑ Ⓒ Ⓓ 15 Ⓐ Ⓑ Ⓒ Ⓓ
             10 Ⓕ Ⓖ Ⓗ Ⓙ 12 Ⓕ Ⓖ Ⓗ Ⓙ 14 Ⓕ Ⓖ Ⓗ Ⓙ 16 Ⓕ Ⓖ Ⓗ Ⓙ

17 What is the correct way to begin a letter?

- Ⓐ Dear Uncle Mark,
- Ⓑ Dear uncle Mark,
- Ⓒ dear uncle Mark,
- Ⓓ Dear Uncle Mark.

18 The computer in our classroom came from _____ .

- Ⓕ Miami. Florida
- Ⓖ Miami Florida
- Ⓗ miami, florida
- Ⓙ Miami, Florida

Read this story and answer questions 19–22. The story has groups of underlined words. The questions will ask about them.

Our neighbors name is Ms. Miller. She is the oldest person in our town. Last
(1)   (2)   (3)
year, she had her hundredth birthday. There was a Big Celebration in the
*   (4)*
town hall. Ms. Miller still walks more than a mile every day she also enjoys
*   (5)*
coming to school and visiting our classes. The children like to ask her what
*   (6)*
the town was like when she was a little girl. Her stories are funny and make
*   (7)*
us glad we weren't around then.

19 In sentence 1, Our neighbors name is best written—

- Ⓐ our neighbors name
- Ⓑ Our neighbors Name
- Ⓒ Our neighbor's name
- Ⓓ as it is

20 In sentence 4, Big Celebration is best written—

- Ⓕ Big celebration
- Ⓖ big celebration
- Ⓗ big Celebration
- Ⓙ as it is

21 In sentence 5, day she also is best written—

- Ⓐ day. She also
- Ⓑ day, she also
- Ⓒ day she also.
- Ⓓ as it is

22 In sentence 6, little girl. is best written—

- Ⓕ little girl?
- Ⓖ little girl!
- Ⓗ little girl,
- Ⓙ as it is

UNIT 2   LANGUAGE EXPRESSION

Lesson 5   Nouns and Pronouns

Examples   **Directions:** For items 1-3, choose the word that best completes the sentence. For items 4-6, choose the answer that could replace the underlined word in the sentence.

A _____ enjoys playing tennis.

- Ⓐ They
- Ⓑ He
- Ⓒ Him
- Ⓓ Them

B <u>Nancy</u> built a bench for the yard.

- Ⓕ She
- Ⓖ Her
- Ⓗ Them
- Ⓙ Us

Tips   If a question is too difficult, skip it and come back to it later.

Choose the answer that fits best in the sentence.

Practice

1 Mary and _____ went to a concert last Saturday.

- Ⓐ her
- Ⓑ him
- Ⓒ me
- Ⓓ I

2 Ask _____ to join us for lunch.

- Ⓕ it
- Ⓖ them
- Ⓗ she
- Ⓙ they

3 What did you tell _____ to bring to the party?

- Ⓐ her
- Ⓑ he
- Ⓒ they
- Ⓓ I

4 Let <u>Manny</u> have a turn using the computer.

- Ⓕ he
- Ⓖ his
- Ⓗ him
- Ⓙ it

5 <u>Joan and Tim</u> built their own house.

- Ⓐ They
- Ⓑ Him
- Ⓒ Her
- Ⓓ Them

6 When did you lose <u>your</u> basketball?

- Ⓕ him
- Ⓖ her
- Ⓗ we
- Ⓙ it

GO

ANSWER ROWS   A Ⓐ Ⓑ Ⓒ Ⓓ   1 Ⓐ Ⓑ Ⓒ Ⓓ   3 Ⓐ Ⓑ Ⓒ Ⓓ   5 Ⓐ Ⓑ Ⓒ Ⓓ
56   B Ⓕ Ⓖ Ⓗ Ⓙ   2 Ⓕ Ⓖ Ⓗ Ⓙ   4 Ⓕ Ⓖ Ⓗ Ⓙ   6 Ⓕ Ⓖ Ⓗ Ⓙ

Lesson 5 Nouns and Pronouns

Examples **Directions:** For items C and 7-8, choose the underlined part of the sentence that is the simple subject. For items D and 9, choose the sentence that contains a complete subject. For items E and 10-11, choose the answer that has a mistake. Mark the space "No mistakes" if there are no errors. For items F-G and 12-15, choose the sentence that is written correctly.

C	A <u>dish</u> <u>fell</u> from the <u>kitchen</u> <u>table</u>.
	Ⓐ Ⓑ Ⓒ Ⓓ

D	Ⓕ	Randy began working <u>in an office</u>.
	Ⓖ	He has to <u>take the train</u> to work.
	Ⓗ	The elevator went <u>quickly</u>.
	Ⓙ	<u>Both phones</u> rang at the same time.

E	Ⓐ	That ball is mine.
	Ⓑ	I lost them last week
	Ⓒ	near the baseball field.
	Ⓓ	(No mistakes)

F	Ⓕ	Dean planted a tree.
	Ⓖ	Visiting a garden store.
	Ⓗ	Between the house and the pond.
	Ⓙ	A shovel and a pick.

G	Ⓐ	A shopping cart near the door.
	Ⓑ	Dropped the milk but not broken.
	Ⓒ	The groceries are in the car.
	Ⓓ	Forgot the bread for dinner.

7 A <u>large</u> black <u>bear</u> <u>walked</u> <u>nearby</u>.
        Ⓐ   Ⓑ   Ⓒ   Ⓓ

8 <u>Patrick's</u> <u>friend</u> gave <u>him</u> a <u>book</u>.
         Ⓕ   Ⓖ   Ⓗ   Ⓙ

9 Ⓐ The lawn <u>needs</u> to be mowed.
   Ⓑ <u>Denise and I</u> washed the car.
   Ⓒ <u>Our</u> mailbox was full.
   Ⓓ The vacation <u>was wonderful</u>.

10 Ⓕ The dogs look thirsty.
    Ⓖ Let's give them water
    Ⓗ before we go outside.
    Ⓙ (No mistakes)

11 Ⓐ Call Andy and Nina.
    Ⓑ Maybe them will want
    Ⓒ to go shopping with us.
    Ⓓ (No mistakes)

12 Ⓕ Him was not happy about losing.
    Ⓖ The game was exciting.
    Ⓗ Me and Tina had good seats.
    Ⓙ The tickets, they were free.

13 Ⓐ Riding through the muddy field.
    Ⓑ Thought it would be fun.
    Ⓒ Then fell and started laughing.
    Ⓓ The bicycles got very dirty.

14 Ⓕ The race will start at the park.
    Ⓖ Running for about half an hour.
    Ⓗ Up the hill then down again.
    Ⓙ Started at ten o'clock.

15 Ⓐ Snowed in summer.
    Ⓑ Surprised by strange weather.
    Ⓒ The date was July 15.
    Ⓓ Remembering it well.

ANSWER ROWS	C Ⓐ Ⓑ Ⓒ Ⓓ	F Ⓕ Ⓖ Ⓗ Ⓙ	8 Ⓕ Ⓖ Ⓗ Ⓙ	11 Ⓐ Ⓑ Ⓒ Ⓓ	14 Ⓕ Ⓖ Ⓗ Ⓙ
	D Ⓕ Ⓖ Ⓗ Ⓙ	G Ⓐ Ⓑ Ⓒ Ⓓ	9 Ⓐ Ⓑ Ⓒ Ⓓ	12 Ⓕ Ⓖ Ⓗ Ⓙ	15 Ⓐ Ⓑ Ⓒ Ⓓ
	E Ⓐ Ⓑ Ⓒ Ⓓ	7 Ⓐ Ⓑ Ⓒ Ⓓ	10 Ⓕ Ⓖ Ⓗ Ⓙ	13 Ⓐ Ⓑ Ⓒ Ⓓ	

Lesson 6   Verbs

Examples **Directions:** For items A and 1-2, choose the word that best completes the sentence. For items 3-4, choose the sentence that is written correctly. For items B and 5-6, look for the sentence that has a mistake. Mark the circle "No mistakes" if there are no errors. For items 7-8, choose the sentence that is written correctly. For items 9-10, mark the circle for the part of each sentence that is a simple predicate.

A   The package _____ yesterday.

- Ⓐ will come
- Ⓒ come
- Ⓑ coming
- Ⓓ came

B
- Ⓕ The kittens is playing
- Ⓖ with the string. They
- Ⓗ are having a good time.
- Ⓙ (No mistakes)

Tips Remember, a verb is an action word.

If you are not sure which answer is correct, take your best guess.

Practice

1   The fireplace _____ the room warm and cozy.

- Ⓐ to keep
- Ⓒ keeps
- Ⓑ keeping
- Ⓓ keep

2   A band _____ in the park next week.

- Ⓕ play
- Ⓗ played
- Ⓖ will play
- Ⓙ was playing

3
- Ⓐ The plane landed safely.
- Ⓑ Our class visit the airport.
- Ⓒ We sitted in the pilot's seat.
- Ⓓ The lunch we had eat was great.

4
- Ⓕ Deena play a computer game.
- Ⓖ The weather are too cold.
- Ⓗ I carried the box to the attic.
- Ⓙ We have did funny things.

5
- Ⓐ The money we saved
- Ⓑ will be used to buy
- Ⓒ a gift for my grandmother.
- Ⓓ (No mistakes)

6
- Ⓕ Stan will hafta wait.
- Ⓖ Martha was here earlier
- Ⓗ so she will play first.
- Ⓙ (No mistakes)

7
- Ⓐ A room for watching videos.
- Ⓑ Books, tapes and magazines.
- Ⓒ The library is open tomorrow.
- Ⓓ Borrowing books to read for school.

8
- Ⓕ Some people tennis all year.
- Ⓖ Which sport do you liking?
- Ⓗ Watching television not a sport.
- Ⓙ Sailing is my favorite sport.

9   The   driver   quickly   stopped   the   car.
           Ⓐ   Ⓑ   Ⓒ   Ⓓ

10   They   came   home   after   the   movie.
            Ⓕ   Ⓖ   Ⓗ   Ⓙ

Lesson 7 Adjectives

Examples

A Who is the _____ runner?

- Ⓐ most fast
- Ⓑ fastest
- Ⓒ more faster
- Ⓓ most fastest

B
- Ⓕ This is a huge mall.
- Ⓖ That was a loudest noise.
- Ⓗ I have a worser pain.
- Ⓙ This glass is fullest than that one.

Tips If you know which answer is correct, mark it and move on to the next item.

Stay with your first answer choice. It is usually right.

Practice

1 The river is _____ now than it is in the fall.

- Ⓐ deep
- Ⓑ most deep
- Ⓒ deepest
- Ⓓ deeper

2 That lamp is _____ .

- Ⓕ brightly
- Ⓖ bright
- Ⓗ most brightest
- Ⓙ more brighter

3 Who is _____ , Ann or Ned?

- Ⓐ most funnior
- Ⓑ funniest
- Ⓒ funnier
- Ⓓ most funny

4 The _____ gift you can give your grandfather is to visit him.

- Ⓕ most wonderful
- Ⓖ wonderfully
- Ⓗ wonderful
- Ⓙ more wonderfuller

5
- Ⓐ The trip to the beach took long than we expected.
- Ⓑ The wind blew more hard.
- Ⓒ This was a most tastier lunch.
- Ⓓ Charlene was busy all weekend with her friends.

6
- Ⓕ He swims slower than Nora.
- Ⓖ The gift is too larger for the box.
- Ⓗ A saddest movie is playing now.
- Ⓙ It is too lately to go to the lake.

7
- Ⓐ A lightest backpack is better than a heaviest one.
- Ⓑ The bus was most crowdeder this morning.
- Ⓒ This is the widest street in town.
- Ⓓ I buy the most ripest fruit.

Lesson 8   Sentences

Examples   Directions: Choose the sentence that is written correctly.

A Ⓐ An apple fell from the tree.
   Ⓑ Stopped to buy fruit.
   Ⓒ The family on a Sunday ride.
   Ⓓ Away from crowded city streets.

B Ⓕ It's time to go we can come again.
   Ⓖ Beside the house near the tree.
   Ⓗ Our neighbors built a pool.
   Ⓙ Your friends called will stop by.

Choose the answer that is the best combination of the underlined sentences.

C Let's go to the zoo.
   Let's go tomorrow morning.

   Ⓐ Let's go tomorrow to the zoo in the morning.
   Ⓑ In the morning, let's go to the zoo tomorrow.
   Ⓒ Let's go to the zoo, and let's go tomorrow morning.
   Ⓓ Let's go to the zoo tomorrow morning.

Tips   Say the answer choices to yourself carefully. Choose the one that sounds the best.

Practice

1 Ⓐ Such a nice day.
   Ⓑ The two friends went for a ride on a boat.
   Ⓒ To do something that we have never tried before.
   Ⓓ A good time all afternoon.

2 Ⓕ The man at the bank helped Kate.
   Ⓖ The money she saved from working.
   Ⓗ Some in the bank each month for a year.
   Ⓙ More than two hundred dollars.

3 Ⓐ Looking for license plates from different states.
   Ⓑ A trip to a national park in Idaho.
   Ⓒ Finally there for a great visit.
   Ⓓ The children were bored because the ride was long.

4 Ⓕ Call before you come we'll be sure to be home.
   Ⓖ The bus will stop at our corner you will see our building.
   Ⓗ Our apartment is on the second floor of the building.
   Ⓙ My mother will drive you home our car will be fixed by then.

GO

Lesson 8   Sentences

Directions: For items 5-6, read the underlined sentences. Choose the answer that is the best combination of the underlined sentences. For items 7-8, choose the word that shows the best way to say the underlined part of each sentence. For items 9-10, choose the sentence that is written correctly.

5   <u>The phone rang four times.</u>

   <u>The phone is in the kitchen.</u>

   Ⓐ   The phone in the kitchen rang four times.

   Ⓑ   The phone is in the kitchen and it rang four times.

   Ⓒ   The phone, it rang four times, and it is in the kitchen.

   Ⓓ   The ringing phone is in the kitchen.

6   <u>Trees surround the lake in the park.</u>

   <u>The trees are tall.</u>

   Ⓕ   Trees surround the lake in the park, and the trees are tall.

   Ⓖ   The trees that surround the lake in the park are tall trees.

   Ⓗ   Tall trees surround the lake in the park.

   Ⓙ   Tall trees that surround the lake are in the park.

---

7   We can go to the movies **after** you finish your homework.

   Ⓐ   since   Ⓑ   but   Ⓒ   and   Ⓓ   *(No change)*

8   The radio she **buyed** was on sale.

   Ⓕ   buy   Ⓖ   bought   Ⓗ   will buy   Ⓙ   *(No change)*

---

9   Ⓐ   Next year a bridge across the river.
   Ⓑ   Across the river, a bridge will be finished.
   Ⓒ   The bridge across the river will be finished next year.
   Ⓓ   The bridge next year will be finished across the river.

10   Ⓕ   Traffic around the stadium was awful because of the big game.
   Ⓖ   The big game and awful traffic around the stadium.
   Ⓗ   Because of the big game, awful traffic around the stadium.
   Ⓙ   Traffic, which was around the stadium, was awful because of the big game.

ANSWER ROWS   5 Ⓐ Ⓑ Ⓒ Ⓓ   7 Ⓐ Ⓑ Ⓒ Ⓓ   9 Ⓐ Ⓑ Ⓒ Ⓓ
               6 Ⓕ Ⓖ Ⓗ Ⓙ   8 Ⓕ Ⓖ Ⓗ Ⓙ   10 Ⓕ Ⓖ Ⓗ Ⓙ

Lesson 8　　Sentences

Read this letter. Use it to answer questions 11–14.

Dear Dr. Baker,

Thank you for taking such good care of me last week. I was afraid and sore
(1)　　　　　　　　　　　　　　　　　　　　　　　　(2)
when I came to the hospital. You made me feel better and fixed my cut. It's
　　　　(3)　　　　　　　　　　　　　　　　　　　　　　　　(4)
getting better. I should be back in school tomorrow. I did everything you told
　　　　　(5)　　　　　　　　　　　　　　(6)
me to and it helped a lot. My parents were surprised at how quickly I am
　　　　　　　　　　　　(7)
improving. They told me, your daughter, who goes to our school. When I go
　　　　　(8)　　　　　　　　　　　　　　　　　　　　　　　　(9)
back to school I will try to find her. Maybe can become friends.
　　　　　　　　　　　　　　　　　　　(10)

11 Sentence 2 is best written—

Ⓐ When I came to the hospital, I was afraid and I was sore.

Ⓑ Afraid and sore, I came to the hospital.

Ⓒ I was afraid when I came to the hospital, and sore.

Ⓓ as it is

12 Sentence 8 is best written—

Ⓕ In our school, they told me you have a daughter.

Ⓖ They told me that your daughter goes to our school.

Ⓗ Your daughter, they told me, who goes to our school.

Ⓙ as it is

13 Which of these is not a sentence?

1　　3　　5　　10
Ⓐ　　Ⓑ　　Ⓒ　　Ⓓ

14 How are sentences 4 and 5 best joined without changing the meaning?

Ⓕ After I get better, I should be back in school tomorrow.

Ⓖ It's getting better, so I should be back in school tomorrow.

Ⓗ Tomorrow, after I am back in school, I should be getting better.

Ⓙ I should, because it's getting better, be back in school tomorrow.

Lesson 9   Paragraphs

Examples **Directions:** Read the paragraph with the blank. Choose the answer that is the best topic sentence for the paragraph.

A _____ . Although it is very thin, it protects our muscles and internal organs. Skin is flexible and can stretch in every direction. In addition, skin is one of the sense organs and lets us feel temperature, pressure, and other things.

- Ⓐ Skin, hair, and fingernails are similar in many ways.
- Ⓑ Our skin is truly amazing.
- Ⓒ The human skin is thinner than the skin of many other animals.
- Ⓓ Skin can be cut or bruised.

Tips Remember, a paragraph should focus on one idea.
Be sure to read all the answer choices.

Practice

1 _____ . Many people think of art as being paintings or statues. It also includes dancing, music, landscape, buildings, and many other practical things. Some of the most beautiful pieces of art are pots, baskets, and even carpets.

- Ⓐ People have enjoyed art for thousands of years.
- Ⓑ Painting is a popular form of art.
- Ⓒ Art can sometimes be hard to understand.
- Ⓓ Art can take many forms.

2 _____ . Whales swim many thousands of miles to where their calves are born. Some fish return to the same stream where they were born to lay their eggs. Even land animals like elk travel great distances to find places where there is plenty of food.

- Ⓕ Birds often fly south for the winter.
- Ⓖ Some animals stay in the same place all year.
- Ⓗ Many animals other than birds migrate from place to place.
- Ⓙ Animals move more than plants.

GO

ANSWER ROWS   **A** Ⓐ Ⓑ Ⓒ Ⓓ   **1** Ⓐ Ⓑ Ⓒ Ⓓ   **2** Ⓕ Ⓖ Ⓗ Ⓙ

63

Lesson 9   Paragraphs

Examples   Directions: For items 3-4, read each topic sentence. Choose the answer that best develops the topic sentence.

3   Banks are important for two reasons.

  Ⓐ It is easy to open a savings account in a bank. The bank will actually pay you to keep money there.

  Ⓑ Money that you put in a bank is very safe. It is protected by the government so you can never lose it.

  Ⓒ The money you put in a bank earns interest. This means that your money increases the longer you keep it in a bank.

  Ⓓ They give people a safe place to keep their money. Banks also lend money to people for things like buying houses or starting businesses.

4   The Martin family went on a dream vacation. _____ . The weather was wonderful and they saw many beautiful places.

  Ⓕ They live in a small town in Iowa.

  Ⓖ They spent a week on a boat sailing from island to island.

  Ⓗ The children couldn't wait to tell their friends about it.

  Ⓙ When they got on the plane, it was cold and snowy.

Use this paragraph to do numbers 5–7.

¹It was the first time I had ever gone to a play. ²After the play, we stopped in a restaurant for dinner. ³My friends and I took the bus to the theater. ⁴We bought our tickets and found our seats. ⁵The play was about a pioneer family. ⁶I liked the play, but I thought it was too long.

5   Choose the best first sentence for this paragraph.

  Ⓐ A play can be exciting, even for children my age.
  Ⓑ Have you ever been to a play?
  Ⓒ On Saturday we went to a play.
  Ⓓ The actors in the play did a wonderful job.

6   Where is the best place for sentence 2?

  Ⓕ Where it is now
  Ⓖ Between sentences 3 and 4
  Ⓗ Between sentences 4 and 5
  Ⓙ After sentence 6

7   Choose the best last sentence for this paragraph.

  Ⓐ If I have a chance, I think I would like to go to another play.
  Ⓑ I was surprised because other children our age were there.
  Ⓒ We met our teacher at the theater.
  Ⓓ My parents asked me to call when we got to the theater.

64   GO

ANSWER ROWS   3 Ⓐ Ⓑ Ⓒ Ⓓ   4 Ⓕ Ⓖ Ⓗ Ⓙ   5 Ⓐ Ⓑ Ⓒ Ⓓ   6 Ⓕ Ⓖ Ⓗ Ⓙ   7 Ⓐ Ⓑ Ⓒ Ⓓ

Read this essay. Use it to answer questions 8–11.

Keeping Warm

There are several things you can do to keep warm. The most important thing (1) (2) is to dress in layers. If you wear long underwear, a sweater, and a coat, you (3) will stay warm in even the coldest weather. Skiing, hiking, and sledding are (4) good ways to enjoy the outdoors in winter. Another good idea is to wear a (5) hat. People lose a lot of body heat through the head. A hat will prevent this. (6) (7) Drinking something warm before you go outside or while you are outside will (8) also help.

8 Which sentence would best begin this essay?

- Ⓕ Most people take their vacation in summer rather than winter.
- Ⓖ If you want to enjoy the outdoors in winter, you must keep warm.
- Ⓗ There are many ways to enjoy the outdoors in winter.
- Ⓙ Being cold is not very much fun.

9 Which of these could be added after sentence 7?

- Ⓐ Wool hats that cover your ears are probably the best.
- Ⓑ Hats don't cost a lot.
- Ⓒ A hat can keep the sun out of your eyes in the summer.
- Ⓓ You can buy a hat almost anywhere.

10 Which sentence does not belong in this essay?

1	3	4	6
Ⓕ	Ⓖ	Ⓗ	Ⓙ

11 Which of these could be added at the end of the essay?

- Ⓐ In the end, it is better to be warm than cold.
- Ⓑ You won't have a good time if you stay inside all winter.
- Ⓒ And don't forget, the days are shorter in winter, so be sure to head back while it is light outside.
- Ⓓ Finally, you should keep dry, because getting wet causes you to lose body heat quickly.

Lesson 10 Test Yourself

Examples Directions: For items E1 and 1-3, choose the word that best fits the sentence. For item 4, choose the pronoun that could replace the underlined word in the sentence. For items E2 and 5-8, choose the sentence that is written correctly.

E1 The turkey _____ ten pounds.

- Ⓐ weigh
- Ⓑ weighs
- Ⓒ weighing
- Ⓓ is weigh

E2
- Ⓕ Clothes on hangers neatly.
- Ⓖ Keeping toys together in a box.
- Ⓗ The door to the closet is open.
- Ⓙ The muddy shoes in the garage.

1 This is the _____ dog I have ever met.

- Ⓐ friendlier
- Ⓑ friendly
- Ⓒ friendliest
- Ⓓ friend

5
- Ⓐ The door behind you.
- Ⓑ The window is open too far.
- Ⓒ Wiping feet on the mat.
- Ⓓ To come in after playing outside.

2 The frogs _____ croaking when we walk by.

- Ⓕ will stop
- Ⓖ are stopping
- Ⓗ stopped
- Ⓙ stops

6
- Ⓕ This computer is more powerful than that one.
- Ⓖ My computer is heavy than yours.
- Ⓗ The game I bought is the most funner.
- Ⓙ My typing is more better because I practice a lot.

3 This car is _____ than that one.

- Ⓐ new
- Ⓑ newer
- Ⓒ most new
- Ⓓ more newer

7
- Ⓐ Nina and José did coming later.
- Ⓑ This bicycle have a nice seat.
- Ⓒ A truck are coming down the road.
- Ⓓ Three planes landed at almost the same time.

4 Ask <u>Jean and Marcus</u> if they can come tomorrow.

- Ⓕ they
- Ⓖ her
- Ⓗ him
- Ⓙ them

8
- Ⓕ Thems brought presents for Suki.
- Ⓖ Have you told he what time to come?
- Ⓗ Ask her to call me tomorrow.
- Ⓙ Give they directions to the party.

Directions: For items 9-13, choose the answer that has a mistake. Mark the space "No mistakes" if there are no errors. For items 14-15, choose the sentence that has the <u>complete subject</u> underlined. For items 16-17, choose the sentence that has the <u>complete predicate</u> underlined. For items 18-19, choose the answer that has the <u>simple subject</u> underlined. For items 20-21, choose the answer that has the <u>simple predicate</u> underlined.

9 Ⓐ The flowers you planted
   Ⓑ are doing well.
   Ⓒ Do you water them often?
   Ⓓ *(No mistakes)*

10 Ⓕ Aunt Marcie called.
   Ⓖ She wants to know if we
   Ⓗ can stay at there house.
   Ⓙ *(No mistakes)*

11 Ⓐ I didn't get no sleep.
   Ⓑ The bed was too soft
   Ⓒ and the wind blew all night long.
   Ⓓ *(No mistakes)*

12 Ⓕ The train is late
   Ⓖ because an car stopped
   Ⓗ on the tracks and got stuck.
   Ⓙ *(No mistakes)*

13 Ⓐ A boat will sail
   Ⓑ from Miami next week
   Ⓒ for a trip to Puerto Rico.
   Ⓓ *(No mistakes)*

14 Ⓕ <u>The cereal is</u> on the table.
   Ⓖ <u>One sandwich</u> is left in the bag.
   Ⓗ You can have <u>the small apple</u>.
   Ⓙ <u>The orange</u> juice is finished.

15 Ⓐ People <u>have many different</u> hobbies.
   Ⓑ <u>Harvey looks</u> for strange rocks.
   Ⓒ An old bottle <u>was found</u> in our attic.
   Ⓓ <u>My friend</u> collects stamps.

16 Ⓕ The ice <u>began</u> to melt.
   Ⓖ Anita <u>will go to the game</u>.
   Ⓗ A letter came <u>for you yesterday</u>.
   Ⓙ <u>The boys washed</u> the dishes.

17 Ⓐ <u>A kind woman</u> helped Uri.
   Ⓑ It was hard <u>to make a decision</u>.
   Ⓒ <u>The train is moving slowly</u>.
   Ⓓ <u>Some paint spilled</u> on the floor.

18 The <u>map</u> <u>shows</u> two <u>ways</u> to go <u>home</u>.
        Ⓕ   Ⓖ   Ⓗ   Ⓙ

19 A <u>friendly</u> <u>cow</u> <u>walked</u> up to the <u>fence</u>.
        Ⓐ   Ⓑ   Ⓒ   Ⓓ

20 They <u>planted</u> a <u>tree</u> in the <u>back</u> <u>yard</u>.
          Ⓕ   Ⓖ   Ⓗ   Ⓙ

21 The <u>group</u> of <u>hikers</u> <u>climbed</u> the <u>steep</u> trail.
         Ⓐ   Ⓑ   Ⓒ   Ⓓ

Lesson 10 Test Yourself

Read this journal entry. Use it to answer questions 22–25.

My cousins Kevin and Melissa came today they will be staying with us for a
(1)
week. They are about my age so we do lots of things together. The last time
       (2)   (3)
they were here. It was in 1992. This time they brought a camcorder with
         (4)   (5)
them. They want to take videos when we go to the lake. Water skiing and a
      (6)   (7)
boat for it. They have never gone water skiing before. I've gone a few times
   (8)   (9)
and can get up pretty well. Mom is a very good water skier. She will be able
                         (10)   (11)
to teach them how to do it.

22 Sentence 1 is best written—

(F) My cousins Kevin and Melissa came today. They will be staying with us for a week.

(G) Today my cousins, who are Kevin and Melissa, came for a week to be staying with us.

(H) Kevin and Melissa, my cousins, came today. For a week to be staying with us.

(J) as it is

23 Sentence 5 is best written—

(A) This time a camcorder with them.

(B) This time they brung a camcorder with them.

(C) The camcorder that they brought with them.

(D) as it is

24 Which of these is not a sentence?

2	7	9	10
(F)	(G)	(H)	(J)

25 How are sentences 3 and 4 best joined without changing the meaning?

(A) In 1992 was the last time they were here.

(B) They were here in 1992 for the last time.

(C) The last time they were here was in 1992.

(D) The last time and they were here and it was in 1992.

68

ANSWER ROWS 22 (F)(G)(H)(J)   23 (A)(B)(C)(D)   24 (F)(G)(H)(J)   25 (A)(B)(C)(D)

Lesson 10 Test Yourself

Directions: For items 26-27, choose the answer that is the best combination of the underlined sentences. For items 28-29, choose the word that could replace the underlined word in the sentence. For items 30-31, choose the sentence that is written correctly.

26 <u>The bank is on Fifth Avenue.</u>

<u>The supermarket is on Fifth Avenue.</u>

- Ⓕ On Fifth Avenue is the bank and also the supermarket.
- Ⓖ The bank is on Fifth Avenue, which is where the supermarket is.
- Ⓗ The bank and the supermarket are on Fifth Avenue.
- Ⓙ The bank is on Fifth Avenue and the supermarket is on Fifth Avenue.

27 <u>Tina will visit her grandfather next week.</u>

<u>Tina's grandfather is in Georgia.</u>

- Ⓐ Tina will visit her grandfather in Georgia next week.
- Ⓑ Tina will visit Georgia next week and her grandfather.
- Ⓒ In Georgia is Tina's grandfather who she will visit.
- Ⓓ Tina's grandfather will be visited by her in Georgia.

28 You can go to the mall, **but** you must call when you get there.

- Ⓕ since
- Ⓖ or
- Ⓗ if
- Ⓙ (No change)

29 The package you were waiting for **coming** yesterday.

- Ⓐ will come
- Ⓑ came
- Ⓒ comes
- Ⓓ (No change)

30
- Ⓕ This time of year for which it is warm.
- Ⓖ It is very warm for this time of year.
- Ⓗ Although it is warm, it is this time of year.
- Ⓙ A warm time of year it is for this.

31
- Ⓐ Having the tools you need before beginning.
- Ⓑ Before you have the tools you should be beginning.
- Ⓒ The tools, which you should be having, before you begin.
- Ⓓ Before you begin, be sure you have all the tools you will need.

GO

ANSWER ROWS   26 Ⓕ Ⓖ Ⓗ Ⓙ   28 Ⓕ Ⓖ Ⓗ Ⓙ   30 Ⓕ Ⓖ Ⓗ Ⓙ
              27 Ⓐ Ⓑ Ⓒ Ⓓ   29 Ⓐ Ⓑ Ⓒ Ⓓ   31 Ⓐ Ⓑ Ⓒ Ⓓ

Lesson 10   Test Yourself

Directions: For item 32, read the paragraph with the blank. Choose the answer that is the best topic sentence for the paragraph. For item 33, read each topic sentence. Choose the answer that best develops the topic sentence. For items 34-35, read the paragraph with the blank. Choose the sentence that best fits in the paragraph.

32 _____ . Some people like running or biking, which are very hard work. Others prefer fishing or golf, which are much easier.

- (F) Many sports require special equipment.
- (G) People enjoy many different kinds of sports.
- (H) Sports can be played in all seasons.
- (J) Soccer is a popular sport around the world.

33 Traffic was terrible yesterday afternoon.

- (A) Cars were backed up from the bridge all the way to the interstate. It took my parents almost an hour to get home from work.
- (B) A truck crashed into the bridge over the river. The driver was not injured, but it will take several months to fix the bridge.
- (C) Normally it takes my parents about twenty minutes to get home. They work near each other and come home from work together.
- (D) The bridge was damaged when a truck crashed into it. The truck was carrying wood and bricks for a new house.

34   We began feeding birds this winter. _____ . The birds enjoy different kinds of seeds, peanuts, and even apples.

- (F) It has snowed more than usual this year.
- (G) Our state bird is the cardinal.
- (H) You can buy bird food at many different stores.
- (J) There isn't much food for them, especially if it snows.

35   My friend Dora lives in the apartment below us. _____ . Dora's parents opened a restaurant just a few blocks from our building.

- (A) Another friend, Seth, lives near school.
- (B) Sometimes it is hard to make friends.
- (C) Her family moved here a few months ago.
- (D) My favorite food is pizza with everything on it.

ANSWER ROWS   **32** (F)(G)(H)(J)   **33** (A)(B)(C)(D)   **34** (F)(G)(H)(J)   **35** (A)(B)(C)(D)

Lesson 10   Test Yourself

Read this letter. Use it to answer questions 36–39.

Dear Mr. Howard,

The old library is small and has too few books. We would like to raise
(1)   (2)
enough money to add space and buy more books and some computers.

One way we are raising money is asking business owners to allow us to sell
(3)
t-shirts outside their stores. We would set up a table near your door and sell
                                                          (4)
our shirts on Saturday. It won't cost you anything and we promise not to
                                         (5)
bother your customers. Our school was named after the woman who was
                                                           (6)
our town's first mayor.

36 Which sentence would best begin this letter?

- (F) Many students want to read books but can't find them.
- (G) Our school is raising money for a new library.
- (H) Our school is one of the oldest in the state.
- (J) Last week I visited your store.

37 Which of these could be added after sentence 4?

- (A) You can play games on computers.
- (B) Friday is a school day.
- (C) My teacher is new to our school this year.
- (D) The table would be set up from nine to four.

38 Which sentence does not belong in this letter?

1	3	5	6
(F)	(G)	(H)	(J)

39 Which of these could be added at the end of the letter?

- (A) We also promise to clean everything up when we are finished.
- (B) She was also the owner of the first store in town.
- (C) Your store is very busy, and we know a lot of people will come to shop on Saturday.
- (D) It doesn't take long to get from our school to your store, so I am sure we will be on time.

71

STOP

ANSWER ROWS 36 Ⓕ Ⓖ Ⓗ Ⓙ   37 Ⓐ Ⓑ Ⓒ Ⓓ   38 Ⓕ Ⓖ Ⓗ Ⓙ   39 Ⓐ Ⓑ Ⓒ Ⓓ   NUMBER RIGHT _____

UNIT 3 SPELLING

Lesson 11 Spelling Skills

Examples Directions: For items A and 1-6, find the word that best fits in the sentence and is spelled correctly. For items B-D and 7-10, look for the word that is spelled incorrectly. Mark the circle "No mistakes" if there are no errors.

A Money is the _____ reason we can't go.
- Ⓐ cheif
- Ⓑ cheaf
- Ⓒ chief
- Ⓓ cheef

B
- Ⓕ fix
- Ⓖ time
- Ⓗ rest
- Ⓙ stiff
- Ⓚ (No mistakes)

C
- Ⓐ stain
- Ⓑ cogh
- Ⓒ again
- Ⓓ window

D We had a <u>snak</u> <u>after</u> the band <u>concert.</u> <u>No mistake</u>
   Ⓕ   Ⓖ   Ⓗ   Ⓙ

Tips Carefully read the directions! In this lesson you must find both correctly and incorrectly spelled words.

Don't look at the words too long or they all look misspelled.

Practice

1 Don't _____ the cat.
- Ⓐ bothr
- Ⓑ bather
- Ⓒ bothur
- Ⓓ bother

2 My dog's tail has a _____ in it.
- Ⓕ curl
- Ⓖ kurl
- Ⓗ cerl
- Ⓙ kerl

3 A _____ was on the road.
- Ⓐ bolder
- Ⓑ bulder
- Ⓒ boulder
- Ⓓ bouldr

4 That's a good _____.
- Ⓕ trik
- Ⓖ trick
- Ⓗ terick
- Ⓙ treck

5 We'll arrive home at about _____.
- Ⓐ nune
- Ⓑ noone
- Ⓒ noon
- Ⓓ noun

6 My phone _____ is in the book.
- Ⓕ number
- Ⓖ nummber
- Ⓗ numbir
- Ⓙ numbber

7
- Ⓐ mask
- Ⓑ feathur
- Ⓒ sorry
- Ⓓ tame
- Ⓔ (No mistakes)

8
- Ⓕ catch
- Ⓖ point
- Ⓗ snail
- Ⓙ both
- Ⓚ (No mistakes)

9
- Ⓐ pony
- Ⓑ faster
- Ⓒ binch
- Ⓓ seed
- Ⓔ (No mistakes)

10
- Ⓕ strange
- Ⓖ fright
- Ⓗ thought
- Ⓙ pound
- Ⓚ (No mistakes)

GO →

Lesson 11 Spelling Skills

Directions: For items 11-19, find the word that is spelled incorrectly. For items 20-24, read the sentence. Look for the word that has a mistake. Mark the circle "No mistakes" if there are no errors.

11 Ⓐ load
    Ⓑ October
    Ⓒ therteen
    Ⓓ myself

12 Ⓕ lettuce
    Ⓖ jelly
    Ⓗ tries
    Ⓙ nobb

13 Ⓐ weke
    Ⓑ harder
    Ⓒ yesterday
    Ⓓ clown

14 Ⓕ earth
    Ⓖ pudle
    Ⓗ broom
    Ⓙ packed

15 Ⓐ baggage
    Ⓑ sighte
    Ⓒ bucket
    Ⓓ basketball

16 Ⓕ root
    Ⓖ merry
    Ⓗ cage
    Ⓙ arive

17 Ⓐ sting
    Ⓑ heard
    Ⓒ messige
    Ⓓ pillow

18 Ⓕ riting
    Ⓖ dove
    Ⓗ roar
    Ⓙ travel

19 Ⓐ pitcher
    Ⓑ rained
    Ⓒ softly
    Ⓓ dailly

20 The drivers were unabel to stop on the icy road. No mistake
        Ⓕ   Ⓖ   Ⓗ   Ⓙ

21 We picked berries on a farm near the river. No mistake
        Ⓐ   Ⓑ   Ⓒ   Ⓓ

22 I filt bad about losing my sister's sweater. No mistake
      Ⓕ   Ⓖ   Ⓗ   Ⓙ

23 Learning about computers is a lot of fun. No mistake
       Ⓐ   Ⓑ   Ⓒ   Ⓓ

24 The water presure in our house is too low. No mistake
         Ⓕ   Ⓖ   Ⓗ   Ⓙ

Lesson 12 Test Yourself

Examples **Directions:** For items E1 and 1-8, find the word that best fits in the sentence and is spelled correctly. For items E2-E4 and 9-13, look for the word that is spelled incorrectly. Mark the circle "No mistakes" if there are no errors.

E1 Can you please make a _____ of this?
- Ⓐ copie
- Ⓑ copee
- Ⓒ kopy
- Ⓓ copy

E2
- Ⓕ table
- Ⓖ strate
- Ⓗ touch
- Ⓙ crisp
- Ⓚ (No mistakes)

E3
- Ⓐ separaite
- Ⓑ speech
- Ⓒ frame
- Ⓓ cause

E4 We continued to drive behind a school bus for a long time. No mistake
    Ⓕ   Ⓖ   Ⓗ   Ⓙ

1 That is a _____ dress.
- Ⓐ kolorful
- Ⓑ colorfill
- Ⓒ colorful
- Ⓓ colorfull

2 This movie is _____ .
- Ⓕ boreing
- Ⓖ borring
- Ⓗ boring
- Ⓙ borng

3 Use the _____ spoon.
- Ⓐ wooden
- Ⓑ woulden
- Ⓒ woden
- Ⓓ woodden

4 Kanisha has been to the museum _____ .
- Ⓕ twoice
- Ⓖ twyce
- Ⓗ twaice
- Ⓙ twice

5 That's a _____ apple.
- Ⓐ tastie
- Ⓑ tasty
- Ⓒ tastey
- Ⓓ taisty

6 When did you _____ ?
- Ⓕ retern
- Ⓖ retorn
- Ⓗ ruturn
- Ⓙ return

7 You gave me _____ advice.
- Ⓐ useful
- Ⓑ usful
- Ⓒ usefull
- Ⓓ usefill

8 How would you _____ this picture?
- Ⓕ describ
- Ⓖ discribe
- Ⓗ describe
- Ⓙ descreib

9
- Ⓐ pretty
- Ⓑ smart
- Ⓒ tough
- Ⓓ younger
- Ⓔ (No mistakes)

10
- Ⓕ train
- Ⓖ poinnt
- Ⓗ certain
- Ⓙ decision
- Ⓚ (No mistakes)

11
- Ⓐ finished
- Ⓑ manage
- Ⓒ saddle
- Ⓓ seade
- Ⓔ (No mistakes)

12
- Ⓕ teacher
- Ⓖ fraight
- Ⓗ mailbox
- Ⓙ admire
- Ⓚ (No mistakes)

13
- Ⓐ tower
- Ⓑ beyond
- Ⓒ planned
- Ⓓ pownd
- Ⓔ (No mistakes)

GO →

ANSWER ROWS E1 Ⓐ Ⓑ Ⓒ Ⓓ   E4 Ⓕ Ⓖ Ⓗ Ⓙ   3 Ⓐ Ⓑ Ⓒ Ⓓ   6 Ⓕ Ⓖ Ⓗ Ⓙ   9 Ⓐ Ⓑ Ⓒ Ⓓ Ⓔ   12 Ⓕ Ⓖ Ⓗ Ⓙ Ⓚ
             E2 Ⓕ Ⓖ Ⓗ Ⓙ Ⓚ 1 Ⓐ Ⓑ Ⓒ Ⓓ   4 Ⓕ Ⓖ Ⓗ Ⓙ   7 Ⓐ Ⓑ Ⓒ Ⓓ   10 Ⓕ Ⓖ Ⓗ Ⓙ Ⓚ 13 Ⓐ Ⓑ Ⓒ Ⓓ Ⓔ
             E3 Ⓐ Ⓑ Ⓒ Ⓓ   2 Ⓕ Ⓖ Ⓗ Ⓙ   5 Ⓐ Ⓑ Ⓒ Ⓓ   8 Ⓕ Ⓖ Ⓗ Ⓙ   11 Ⓐ Ⓑ Ⓒ Ⓓ Ⓔ

Lesson 12   Test Yourself

Directions: For items 14-22, find the word that is spelled incorrectly. For items 23-27, look for the word that is spelled incorrectly. Mark the circle "No mistakes" if there are no errors.

14 Ⓕ donate   17 Ⓐ peeceful   20 Ⓕ morning
    Ⓖ first   Ⓑ nearly   Ⓖ lucky
    Ⓗ uncle   Ⓒ kind   Ⓗ guard
    Ⓙ thinkt   Ⓓ swimmer   Ⓙ playce

15 Ⓐ answer   18 Ⓕ report   21 Ⓐ fingur
    Ⓑ adress   Ⓖ steer   Ⓑ puzzle
    Ⓒ having   Ⓗ rownd   Ⓒ right
    Ⓓ station   Ⓙ child   Ⓓ crush

16 Ⓕ tipe   19 Ⓐ borrow   22 Ⓕ sheet
    Ⓖ without   Ⓑ workd   Ⓖ basemint
    Ⓗ hidden   Ⓒ story   Ⓗ office
    Ⓙ flew   Ⓓ scrub   Ⓙ dirty

23 Of cours you can stay for dinner. No mistake
       Ⓐ   Ⓑ   Ⓒ   Ⓓ

24 The largest tree will be difficult to climb. No mistake
          Ⓕ   Ⓖ   Ⓗ   Ⓙ

25 Each machene has a special key. No mistake
     Ⓐ   Ⓑ   Ⓒ   Ⓓ

26 Did somone try to complete the form? No mistake
        Ⓕ   Ⓖ   Ⓗ   Ⓙ

27 Wendy droppded the box before I was ready. No mistake
      Ⓐ   Ⓑ   Ⓒ   Ⓓ

UNIT 4 STUDY SKILLS

Lesson 13 Study Skills

Examples Directions: Read each question. Fill in the circle for the answer you think is correct.

A Which of these words comes first in alphabetical order?

- Ⓐ tin
- Ⓑ toy
- Ⓒ table
- Ⓓ trick

B Where would you look to find the most information about sailing?

- Ⓕ in an encyclopedia
- Ⓖ in a dictionary
- Ⓗ in a history book
- Ⓙ in a newspaper

Tips Read each question carefully. Look at any reference materials that are part of the question. Then look at all the answer choices. Choose the one you think is right.

Practice

Marianne was reading a book about art for a group project. Use this Table of Contents and Index to answer numbers 1-3. They are from the art book Marianne is reading.

Table of Contents

Chapter 1	History	1
Chapter 2	Different Types of Art	25
Chapter 3	Famous Artists	43
Chapter 4	Enjoying Art	52
Chapter 5	Becoming an Artist	74

Index

cave paintings	1, 5–8
famous statues	23, 29-31
modern art	24
museums	
American	62-64
European	58-61
Georgia O'Keefe	50
Pablo Picasso	49

1 Marianne can find information about modern art on page—

- Ⓐ 23
- Ⓑ 24
- Ⓒ 49
- Ⓓ 74

2 Information about famous statues can be found on all these pages *except*—

- Ⓕ 23
- Ⓖ 30
- Ⓗ 31
- Ⓙ 32

3 To find out when people first began to create art, Marianne should read Chapter—

- Ⓐ 1
- Ⓑ 3
- Ⓒ 4
- Ⓓ 5

STOP

ANSWER ROWS A Ⓐ Ⓑ Ⓒ Ⓓ   1 Ⓐ Ⓑ Ⓒ Ⓓ   3 Ⓐ Ⓑ Ⓒ Ⓓ
76   B Ⓕ Ⓖ Ⓗ Ⓙ   2 Ⓕ Ⓖ Ⓗ Ⓙ

Lesson 13 Study Skills

Directions: Use the picture dictionary on the left side of the page to do items 4-9.

celebrate
To celebrate is to remember an event with special activities.

currency
Coins and bills used as money are currency.

fox
A fox is a wild animal in the dog family.

hippopotamus
A hippopotamus is a large African animal that lives near water.

karate
Karate is a method of self-defense invented in Japan.

nutrition
The study of the value of different kinds of foods is nutrition.

recover
To recover is to get better after being sick.

---

4 Which word best fits in the sentence, "Quincy saw a _____ in the river when he visited Africa"?

- Ⓕ fox
- Ⓖ hippopotamus
- Ⓗ currency
- Ⓙ celebrate

5 How do you spell the word that means "a method of self-defense"?

- Ⓐ karete
- Ⓑ kerate
- Ⓒ kurate
- Ⓓ karate

6 Which word best fits in the sentence, "Carl read a book about _____ so he would know which foods were best"?

- Ⓕ recover
- Ⓖ celebrate
- Ⓗ nutrition
- Ⓙ currency

7 How do you spell the word that means "coins and bills used as money"?

- Ⓐ currency
- Ⓑ curency
- Ⓒ currincy
- Ⓓ currencie

8 Which of these words go together best?

- Ⓕ eat nutrition
- Ⓖ recover quickly
- Ⓗ angry currency
- Ⓙ celebrate against

9 Which word best fits in the sentence, "When will Agnes _____ from her cold"?

- Ⓐ nutrition
- Ⓑ celebrate
- Ⓒ fox
- Ⓓ recover

ANSWER ROWS 4 Ⓕ Ⓖ Ⓗ Ⓙ   6 Ⓕ Ⓖ Ⓗ Ⓙ   8 Ⓕ Ⓖ Ⓗ Ⓙ
5 Ⓐ Ⓑ Ⓒ Ⓓ   7 Ⓐ Ⓑ Ⓒ Ⓓ   9 Ⓐ Ⓑ Ⓒ Ⓓ

In numbers 10-14, which word comes first in alphabetical order?

10
- Ⓕ hurry
- Ⓖ help
- Ⓗ house
- Ⓙ high

11
- Ⓐ again
- Ⓑ another
- Ⓒ action
- Ⓓ asleep

12
- Ⓕ this
- Ⓖ touch
- Ⓗ trip
- Ⓙ toast

13
- Ⓐ bread
- Ⓑ best
- Ⓒ boat
- Ⓓ blink

14
- Ⓕ open
- Ⓖ owe
- Ⓗ oven
- Ⓙ old

15 Look at these guide words from a dictionary page.

nice—note

Which word would be found on the page?

- Ⓐ noise
- Ⓑ nap
- Ⓒ now
- Ⓓ neither

16 Look at these guide words from a dictionary page.

count—crisp

Which word would be found on the page?

- Ⓕ collect
- Ⓖ celebrate
- Ⓗ crane
- Ⓙ crow

Use the sample dictionary entries and the Pronunciation Guide below to answer numbers 17-19.

heal [hēl] *v.* 1. to make whole; restore to health   2. to bring to an end   3. to purify   4. to cure
health [helth] *n.*   1. the condition of the body or mind   2. freedom from disease
heap [hēp]   1. *n.* a group of things lying on one another   2. *v.* to put things in a pile

Pronunciation Guide:
act, wāy, dâre, ärt, set, ēqual, big, īce, box, ōver, hôrse, bo͝ok, to͞ol, us, tûrn; ə = a in *alone*, e in *mitten*, o in *actor*, u in *circus*

17 The word health sounds most like the word—

- Ⓐ here
- Ⓑ learn
- Ⓒ set
- Ⓓ beach

18 Which definition best fits the word heal as it is used in the sentence below?

A bridge will heal the traffic problem.

1 2 3 4
Ⓕ Ⓖ Ⓗ Ⓙ

19 The word heap sounds most like the word—

- Ⓐ let
- Ⓑ date
- Ⓒ help
- Ⓓ deep

Lesson 14   Test Yourself

Examples   Directions: Read each question. Fill in the circle for the answer you think is correct.

E1 Which of these words comes <u>first</u> in alphabetical order?

- Ⓐ bend
- Ⓑ bush
- Ⓒ brick
- Ⓓ boat

E2 Which one of these is a main heading that includes the other three words?

- Ⓕ Apple
- Ⓖ Peach
- Ⓗ Fruit
- Ⓙ Orange

Directions: For items 1-4, carefully read the question in each item in order to choose the correct answer.

1 Which of these would tell you the page on which the chapters of a book start?

- Ⓐ the index
- Ⓑ the table of contents
- Ⓒ the bibliography
- Ⓓ the title page

2 Which of these would tell you how to break the word <u>tomorrow</u> into syllables?

- Ⓕ an atlas
- Ⓖ an encyclopedia
- Ⓗ a mathematics book
- Ⓙ a dictionary

3 Which of these would tell you the name, address, and telephone number of the restaurants in your town?

- Ⓐ a dictionary
- Ⓑ a cookbook
- Ⓒ a telephone book
- Ⓓ an atlas

4 Which one of these is a main heading that includes the other three words?

- Ⓕ Clothes
- Ⓖ Hat
- Ⓗ Coat
- Ⓙ Shirt

The table of contents below is from a book called *Homes for Americans*. Use it to answer numbers 5 and 6.

Homes for Americans
Table of Contents

Chapter	Page
1 Caves: The First Homes	1
2 Native American Dwellings	12
3 Cold-weather Homes	25
4 Movable Homes	43
5 Palaces in Mexico	59
6 Homes in South America	68
7 Homes of European Settlers	71
8 Building Today and Tomorrow	83
9 Great American Homes	94

5 Which chapter might tell you about the homes of people near the North Pole?

- Ⓐ 1
- Ⓑ 3
- Ⓒ 6
- Ⓓ 8

6 Chapter 8 might tell us about

- Ⓕ the weather tomorrow.
- Ⓖ houses in the desert.
- Ⓗ Civil War homes.
- Ⓙ future ways to build homes.

GO

Lesson 14

In numbers 7-11, which word comes first in alphabetical order?

7 Ⓐ much Ⓒ mouse
   Ⓑ most Ⓓ merry

8 Ⓕ vest Ⓗ valley
   Ⓖ vote Ⓙ village

9 Ⓐ deep Ⓒ dull
   Ⓑ dial Ⓓ dove

10 Ⓕ send Ⓗ shore
   Ⓖ soon Ⓙ scratch

11 Ⓐ north Ⓒ nine
   Ⓑ need Ⓓ numb

12 Look at these guide words from a dictionary page.

   letter—line

   Which word would be found on the page?

   Ⓕ like   Ⓗ lunch
   Ⓖ lead   Ⓙ list

13 Look at these guide words from a dictionary page.

   bath—brick

   Which word would be found on the page?

   Ⓐ bad   Ⓒ brush
   Ⓑ brand Ⓓ by

Use the sample dictionary entries and the Pronunciation Guide below to answer numbers 14-15.

ex • press [ik spres′] *v.* 1. to put into words 2. to show or reveal 3. to send quickly *adj.* 4. clear or easily understood 5. quick *n.* 6. a direct train
ex • pres • sion [ik spresh′ ən] *n.* 1. the act of saying something 2. a special way of saying something

Pronunciation Guide:
act, wāy, dâre, ärt, set, ēqual, big, īce, box, ōver, hôrse, bŏok, to͞ol, us, tûrn; ə = a in *alone*, e in *mitten*, o in *actor*, u in *circus*

14 What is the correct way to divide expression into syllables?

   Ⓕ exp—res—sion
   Ⓖ expres—sion
   Ⓗ ex—pres—sion
   Ⓙ express—ion

15 Which definition best fits the word express as it is used in the sentence below?

   The express will get us home quickly.

   1   2   5   6
   Ⓐ   Ⓑ   Ⓒ   Ⓓ

STOP

Name and Answer Sheet

To the Student:

These tests will give you a chance to put the tips you have learned to work.

A few last reminders…

- Be sure you understand all the directions before you begin each test. You may ask the teacher questions about the directions if you do not understand them.
- Work as quickly as you can during each test.
- When you change an answer, be sure to erase your first mark completely.

- You can guess at an answer or skip difficult items and go back to them later.
- Use the tips you have learned whenever you can.
- It is OK to be a little nervous. You may even do better.

Now that you have completed the lessons in this unit, you are on your way to scoring high!

81

PART 1 LANGUAGE MECHANICS

(Answer bubble sheet — not transcribed)

PART 2 LANGUAGE EXPRESSION

(Answer bubble sheet — not transcribed)

PART 3 SPELLING

(Answer bubble sheet — not transcribed)

PART 4 STUDY SKILLS

(Answer bubble sheet — not transcribed)

UNIT 5   TEST PRACTICE

Part 1   Language Mechanics

Directions: For items E1 and 1-3, read the sentences that are divided into parts. Fill in the circle for the part that has a word that should begin with a capital letter. For items 4-5, choose the answer that fits best in the blank and has the correct capitalization. For items E2 and 6-8, fill in the circle for the punctuation mark that is needed in the sentence. Choose "None" if no punctuation is needed.

E1	When will	you move	to your new house?	None
	Ⓐ	Ⓑ	Ⓒ	Ⓓ

E2	The cars, trucks, and buses moved slowly
	Ⓕ . Ⓖ ? Ⓗ ! Ⓙ None

1. In oregon | there are | many forests. | None
   Ⓐ   Ⓑ   Ⓒ   Ⓓ

2. Both of my sisters | played basketball | in high school. | None
   Ⓕ   Ⓖ   Ⓗ   Ⓙ

3. The weather | last april | was warmer than usual. | None
   Ⓐ   Ⓑ   Ⓒ   Ⓓ

---

4. A flock of birds landed in _____ .
   - Ⓕ the Tall tree
   - Ⓖ the tall Tree
   - Ⓗ the tall tree
   - Ⓙ the Tall Tree

5. Turn right _____ and drive for three more miles.
   - Ⓐ at Riverside Park
   - Ⓑ at riverside park
   - Ⓒ at Riverside park
   - Ⓓ at riverside Park

---

6. Have you finished your homework yet?
   Ⓕ !   Ⓖ .   Ⓗ ,   Ⓙ None

7. Is that your friend's bicycle
   Ⓐ .   Ⓑ !   Ⓒ ?   Ⓓ None

8. Ruth jumped into a pile of leaves
   Ⓕ .   Ⓖ !   Ⓗ ?   Ⓙ None

Part 1 Language Mechanics

Directions: For item 9, choose the answer that you think is correct. For item 10, choose the answer that fits best in the blank and has the correct punctuation.

9 Which is the correct way to begin a letter to a friend of your parents?

- Ⓐ Dear Mr Morris,
- Ⓑ Dear Mr. Morris
- Ⓒ Dear Mr Morris
- Ⓓ Dear Mr. Morris,

10 The children _____ able to eat all the pizza.

- Ⓕ werent
- Ⓖ were'nt
- Ⓗ weren't
- Ⓙ werent'

Directions: For items 11-12, find the answer choice that has a punctuation mistake. Mark the circle "No mistakes" if there are no errors.

11
- Ⓐ "Will you be able
- Ⓑ to find one for me?" Nancy
- Ⓒ asked the store clerk.
- Ⓓ (No mistakes)

12
- Ⓕ Which of these colors
- Ⓖ do you think
- Ⓗ is the prettiest
- Ⓙ (No mistakes)

Directions: For items 13-14, find the answer choice that has correct punctuation and capitalization.

13
- Ⓐ We can build a tree house.
- Ⓑ The children asked their parents if they could borrow some tools
- Ⓒ it took them a few days to finish the tree house.
- Ⓓ How can i help?

14
- Ⓕ Have you read Better Health
- Ⓖ The book Space Adventure will become a movie.
- Ⓗ The Biggest river is a great book.
- Ⓙ Judy Harlan wrote Only Child

Directions: For items 15-16, read the letter. Find the answer choice that shows the correct capitalization and punctuation for the underlined parts.

(15) October 29 1994,

Dear Aunt Millie,

(16) I'm sorry to hear you have been sick. I hope you get well soon so we can play tennis again.

Your nephew,
Bruce

15
- Ⓐ October 29 1994
- Ⓑ October 29, 1994
- Ⓒ October, 29, 1994
- Ⓓ correct as it is

16
- Ⓕ sick I
- Ⓖ sick, I
- Ⓗ sick. i
- Ⓙ correct as it is

17 The factory was first opened on _____ .

- Ⓐ january 4, 1908
- Ⓑ January, 4, 1908
- Ⓒ january, 4, 1908
- Ⓓ January 4, 1908

18 The house on the corner was bought by _____ .

- Ⓕ A. N. Wise
- Ⓖ A N Wise
- Ⓗ a n wise
- Ⓙ a. n. wise

Read this story and answer questions 19–22. The story has groups of underlined words. The questions will ask about them.

Our fishing trip started out fine. We got to the boat around six oclock in the
(1) (2)
morning and headed from shore about 30 minutes later, we stopped the boat

and began to fish. We caught a few fish and were having a Good Time.
(3)
Then the wind started to blow, and it got cloudy. Soon it began to rain. We
(4) (5) (6)
headed back to the dock, but the rain got worse. By the time we reached the
(7)
dock, we were cold, wet, and tired.

19 In sentence 2, six oclock is best written—

- Ⓐ Six Oclock
- Ⓑ six o'clock
- Ⓒ Six O'clock
- Ⓓ as it is

21 In sentence 3, Good Time is best written—

- Ⓐ good Time
- Ⓑ Good time
- Ⓒ good time
- Ⓓ as it is

20 In sentence 2, shore about is best written—

- Ⓕ shore. About
- Ⓖ shore. about
- Ⓗ shore, about
- Ⓙ as it is

22 In sentence 7, cold, wet, and tired is best written—

- Ⓕ cold wet and tired
- Ⓖ cold, wet, and, tired
- Ⓗ cold, wet and tired
- Ⓙ as it is

Part 2 Language Expression

Directions: For items E1 and 1-3, find the word that fits best in the blank. For item 4, read the sentence. Find the pronoun that can replace the underlined word. For items E2 and 5-8, fill in the circle for the answer choice that is a complete and correctly written sentence.

E1 It is too _____ to walk to the store.

- Ⓐ farther
- Ⓑ farthest
- Ⓒ more farther
- Ⓓ far

E2
- Ⓕ Lynne lost her gloves.
- Ⓖ Dwayne and me will be late.
- Ⓗ Them are not my friends.
- Ⓙ This is you seat.

1 The children _____ the steps to the top of the tower.

- Ⓐ climbs
- Ⓑ is climbing
- Ⓒ climbed
- Ⓓ was climbing

2 The _____ flowers are on the plant near the wall.

- Ⓕ prettiest
- Ⓖ prettier
- Ⓗ more pretty
- Ⓙ most prettiest

3 You can lend _____ your hat.

- Ⓐ she
- Ⓑ her
- Ⓒ he
- Ⓓ its

4 Is <u>Emmet</u> going to meet us at the picnic?

- Ⓕ he
- Ⓖ him
- Ⓗ his
- Ⓙ them

5
- Ⓐ Garage door opening slowly.
- Ⓑ Packing things in the trunk.
- Ⓒ Mia and her father this afternoon.
- Ⓓ The car ran out of gas.

6
- Ⓕ An owl flew fastly from a tree.
- Ⓖ The woods seem quiet tonight.
- Ⓗ We walked more slower because it was so dark.
- Ⓙ This is a very brightest flashlight.

7
- Ⓐ Give we a good map.
- Ⓑ We can borrow hims paddles.
- Ⓒ He and I are planning a canoe trip.
- Ⓓ Them will not be able to find us tomorrow.

8
- Ⓕ Our town is growed this year.
- Ⓖ My mother working on Hill Street.
- Ⓗ The parade always start at the park.
- Ⓙ This new store opened last week.

GO

86

Part 2 Language Expression

Directions: For items 9-13, find the answer choice that has a mistake. Mark the circle "No mistakes" if there are no errors. For items 14-15, find the sentence that has the complete subject underlined. For items 16-17, mark the sentence that has the complete predicate underlined. For items 18-19, find the simple subject of the sentence. For items 20-21, find the simple predicate of the sentence.

9
- Ⓐ There ain't no way
- Ⓑ we can get to the post office
- Ⓒ before it closes.
- Ⓓ (No mistakes)

10
- Ⓕ Cassie called. She wants
- Ⓖ to know if you can
- Ⓗ meet her at the pool.
- Ⓙ (No mistakes)

11
- Ⓐ School will be closed
- Ⓑ next week. My family will
- Ⓒ go camping near an lake.
- Ⓓ (No mistakes)

12
- Ⓕ The box you have is
- Ⓖ largest than the ones
- Ⓗ Warren and I brought.
- Ⓙ (No mistakes)

13
- Ⓐ The boots she bought
- Ⓑ wasn't the right size.
- Ⓒ She had to return them.
- Ⓓ (No mistakes)

14
- Ⓕ A truck delivered our <u>new stove</u>.
- Ⓖ <u>Many cars are</u> built in Michigan.
- Ⓗ A large rock <u>fell on the road</u>.
- Ⓙ <u>Four vans</u> are in the lot.

15
- Ⓐ <u>The blue towel</u> is still wet.
- Ⓑ The clothes are <u>drying</u> on the line.
- Ⓒ We <u>should wash</u> the sheets today.
- Ⓓ The <u>soap spilled</u> on the floor.

16
- Ⓕ <u>The farmer</u> plowed the field.
- Ⓖ The barn <u>door swung</u> open.
- Ⓗ The corn <u>grew quickly</u>.
- Ⓙ Her father bought a <u>farm</u>.

17
- Ⓐ Your letter arrived <u>yesterday</u>.
- Ⓑ They <u>will come tomorrow</u>.
- Ⓒ The <u>boat sank</u> quickly.
- Ⓓ We walked <u>on the beach</u>.

18 The <u>picture</u> of a <u>lake</u> was <u>hanging</u> on the <u>wall</u>.
         Ⓕ   Ⓖ   Ⓗ   Ⓙ

19 <u>Two</u> large <u>men</u> carried the <u>sofa</u> into the <u>house</u>.
      Ⓐ   Ⓑ   Ⓒ   Ⓓ

20 <u>Lightning</u> <u>hit</u> the <u>tree</u> by the <u>barn</u>.
         Ⓕ   Ⓖ   Ⓗ   Ⓙ

21 My <u>sister's</u> <u>team</u> <u>won</u> the <u>championship</u>.
             Ⓐ   Ⓑ   Ⓒ   Ⓓ

87

Part 2   Language Expression

Read this essay. Use it to answer questions 22–25.

The earth is part of the solar system. The sun is in the center of the solar
(1)   (2)
system the planets revolve around it. There are nine planets. Mercury is the
                                                     (3)   (4)
closest planet to the sun. The earth is the third planet from the sun. Saturn is
                    (5)   (6)
different from the other planets. It has visible rings. The rings of dust and
                                                        (7)   (8)
small rocks. You can see the rings if you use a telescope or even good
     (9)
binoculars. Many of the planets have moons. The earth has one moon, but
              (10)   (11)
some other planets may have as many as twenty moons.

22 Sentence 2 is best written—

Ⓕ The sun is in the center, the planets revolve around it.

Ⓖ The planets, revolving around the sun, which is at the center of the solar system.

Ⓗ The sun is in the center of the solar system. The planets revolve around it.

Ⓙ as it is

23 Which of these could be added after sentence 4?

Ⓐ Pluto is farthest from the sun.

Ⓑ Planets are made up of different substances.

Ⓒ A moon is not a planet.

Ⓓ The sun is a star.

24 Which of these is not a sentence?

3   5   8   10
Ⓕ   Ⓖ   Ⓗ   Ⓙ

25 How are sentences 6 and 7 best joined without changing the meaning?

Ⓐ Saturn is different from the other planets, and it has visible rings.

Ⓑ Saturn is different from the other planets because it has visible rings.

Ⓒ The visible rings it has, which make Saturn different from the other planets.

Ⓓ The visible rings of Saturn, which it has, make it different from the other planets.

88

Part 2 Language Expression

Directions: Read the underlined sentences. Choose the answer that is the best combination of the sentences.

26 A group of children went to the park.

  A group of children had a picnic.

- Ⓕ A group of children, going to the park, had a picnic.
- Ⓖ A group of children went to the park and had a picnic.
- Ⓗ A group of children, who had a picnic, went to the park.
- Ⓙ A group of children going to the park and having a picnic.

Directions: Read the sentence. Choose the answer that shows the best way to write the underlined part. Mark the circle "No change" if the part is correct.

27 Next summer, I **was visit** my friend in Ohio.

- Ⓐ will visit
- Ⓑ visits
- Ⓒ to visit
- Ⓓ *(No change)*

Directions: Mark the circle for the sentence that is correctly formed.

28
- Ⓕ We couldn't find the brushes, so we painted the porch.
- Ⓖ It was the porch we wanted to paint, if we could find the brushes.
- Ⓗ We wanted to paint the porch, but we couldn't find the brushes.
- Ⓙ Although we couldn't find the brushes, we painted the porch.

Directions: Find the answer choice that is the best topic sentence for the story.

29 _____ . When my sister practices the piano, Molly sings along. Molly sits beside the piano and howls until Elena chases her away.

- Ⓐ My dog Molly is four years old.
- Ⓑ My dog Molly does something very funny.
- Ⓒ My sister plays the piano.
- Ⓓ Dogs can learn many interesting tricks.

Directions: Find the answer choice that best fits the paragraph.

30 The roof of our house started leaking yesterday. _____ . He and my mother will try to fix it today.

- Ⓕ Our house is over a hundred years old.
- Ⓖ The weather has been cold and snowy for weeks.
- Ⓗ My father thinks it was caused by ice.
- Ⓙ My father often repairs our car.

Part 3 Spelling

Examples Directions: For items E1 and 1-8, find the word that is spelled correctly. For items E2-E3 and 9-13, mark the space for the misspelled word.

E1

Don't make any
_____ movements.

- Ⓐ suddin
- Ⓑ sudden
- Ⓒ suden
- Ⓓ suddinn

E2
- Ⓕ thick
- Ⓖ lunch
- Ⓗ nobody
- Ⓙ ladder
- Ⓚ *(No mistakes)*

E3
- Ⓐ main
- Ⓑ sign
- Ⓒ partey
- Ⓓ trunk

---

1 You can play _____ this afternoon.
- Ⓐ toogether
- Ⓑ togethir
- Ⓒ togather
- Ⓓ together

2 Your socks don't _____ .
- Ⓕ mach
- Ⓖ match
- Ⓗ madch
- Ⓙ madtch

3 Practice will _____ __ your swimming.
- Ⓐ improve
- Ⓑ improv
- Ⓒ impruv
- Ⓓ impruve

4 _____ way did the rabbit run?
- Ⓕ Wich
- Ⓖ Whitch
- Ⓗ Widch
- Ⓙ Which

5 Her horse is _____ .
- Ⓐ gentl
- Ⓑ gentle
- Ⓒ gentel
- Ⓓ gentul

6 Mark gave a _____ answer.
- Ⓕ polite
- Ⓖ polit
- Ⓗ polyte
- Ⓙ poleite

7 This is my _____ restaurant.
- Ⓐ favrit
- Ⓑ favrite
- Ⓒ favorite
- Ⓓ favorit

8 The new bank looks very _____ .
- Ⓕ modrn
- Ⓖ moddern
- Ⓗ modern
- Ⓙ modren

9
- Ⓐ chickin
- Ⓑ pattern
- Ⓒ honest
- Ⓓ waste
- Ⓔ *(No mistakes)*

10
- Ⓕ silly
- Ⓖ oposite
- Ⓗ bunch
- Ⓙ worn
- Ⓚ *(No mistakes)*

11
- Ⓐ stretch
- Ⓑ leave
- Ⓒ beside
- Ⓓ readey
- Ⓔ *(No mistakes)*

12
- Ⓕ pitch
- Ⓖ dull
- Ⓗ airrport
- Ⓙ large
- Ⓚ *(No mistakes)*

13
- Ⓐ build
- Ⓑ making
- Ⓒ windy
- Ⓓ respect
- Ⓔ *(No mistakes)*

GO

Part 3 Spelling

Directions: For items 14-22, find the word that is spelled incorrectly. For items 23-27, read the sentence. Mark the space for the word that is spelled incorrectly. Mark the space for "No mistakes" if there are no errors.

14
- F clevir
- G unfair
- H lived
- J rain

15
- A heart
- B oldist
- C funny
- D attach

16
- F easy
- G cover
- H happy
- J repare

17
- A rocky
- B control
- C defind
- D bridge

18
- F several
- G huge
- H mountin
- J fault

19
- A trace
- B frend
- C loud
- D every

20
- F again
- G welcome
- H lettr
- J disobey

21
- A parrtly
- B float
- C visitor
- D cheek

22
- F everybody
- G unless
- H smooth
- J choyce

23 My <u>sister</u> had to <u>rush</u> <u>aftr</u> the bus. <u>No mistake</u>
       (A)   (B)   (C)   (D)

24 How <u>many</u> <u>poeple</u> will the pot of soup <u>serve?</u> <u>No mistake</u>
            (F)   (G)   (H)   (J)

25 Be <u>caerful</u> and drive a <u>little</u> <u>slower.</u> <u>No mistake</u>
          (A)   (B)   (C)   (D)

26 We had to <u>laugh</u> at the <u>kitten</u> under the <u>chair.</u> <u>No mistake</u>
                 (F)   (G)   (H)   (J)

27 You got the <u>highist</u> <u>grade</u> in the <u>class.</u> <u>No mistake</u>
                   (A)   (B)   (C)   (D)

91

Part 4 Study Skills

Examples Directions: Read each question. Fill in the circle for the answer you think is correct.

E1 Which of these words comes first in alphabetical order?

Ⓐ after
Ⓑ against
Ⓒ among
Ⓓ about

E2 Which one of these is a main heading that includes the other three words?

Ⓕ Lunch
Ⓖ Meals
Ⓗ Dinner
Ⓙ Breakfast

---

assist

To assist is to give help or aid.

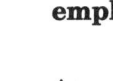

employee

An employee is a person who works for a company.

imitate

To imitate is to act like another person.

pelican

A pelican is a bird that has a large bill and eats fish.

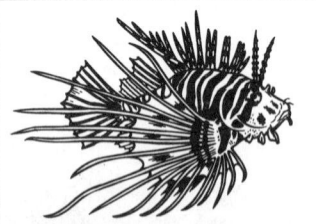

spiny

To be spiny is to be covered with sharp spines.

talented

To be talented is to be able to do things well.

On this page there are pictures and words from a picture dictionary. Use them to answer the questions below.

1 Which word best fits in the sentence, "Teena _____ the way her mother played tennis"?

Ⓐ arrived
Ⓑ talented
Ⓒ imitated
Ⓓ assisted

2 How do you spell the word that means "to help someone"?

Ⓕ assist
Ⓖ asist
Ⓗ assissst
Ⓙ asisst

3 Which of these words go together best?

Ⓐ spiny pelican
Ⓑ assisted spiny
Ⓒ pelican imitated
Ⓓ talented employee

4 How do you spell the word that means "someone who works for a company"?

Ⓕ empleyee
Ⓖ employye
Ⓗ employ
Ⓙ employee

GO

92

Part 4   Study Skills

Directions: For items 12-16, carefully read the question in each item in order to choose the correct answer.

In numbers 5-9, which word comes first in alphabetical order?

5   Ⓐ crash   Ⓒ chicken
     Ⓑ cent   Ⓓ care

6   Ⓕ west   Ⓗ wore
     Ⓖ write   Ⓙ wind

7   Ⓐ friend   Ⓒ flint
     Ⓑ fourth   Ⓓ float

8   Ⓕ roast   Ⓗ rust
     Ⓖ risk   Ⓙ rope

9   Ⓐ north   Ⓒ nine
     Ⓑ need   Ⓓ near

---

10   Look at these guide words from a dictionary page.

     | very—vote |

     Which word would be found on the page?

     Ⓕ voice   Ⓗ vow
     Ⓖ van   Ⓙ vulture

11   Look at these guide words from a dictionary page.

     | lime—lose |

     Which word would be found on the page?

     Ⓐ like   Ⓒ list
     Ⓑ luck   Ⓓ leak

12   Which of these would you use to find the date of Thanksgiving this year?

     Ⓕ a dictionary
     Ⓖ a catalog
     Ⓗ a calendar
     Ⓙ a telephone book

13   Which of these books would give you ideas about where you could take a camping vacation?

     Ⓐ *Making A Campfire*
     Ⓑ *Inexpensive Vacations*
     Ⓒ *Fishing and Hunting*
     Ⓓ *Campgrounds in America*

14   Suppose your teacher asked you to write about your favorite person. Which of these would be most helpful before you begin to write?

     Ⓕ Think about some people you like
     Ⓖ Think about your favorite pet
     Ⓗ Draw a picture of someone
     Ⓙ Write a note to a friend

15   Which one of these is a main heading that includes the other three words?

     Ⓐ Fish
     Ⓑ Pets
     Ⓒ Cats
     Ⓓ Birds

16   Which one of these is a main heading that includes the other three words?

     Ⓕ Flowers
     Ⓖ Rose
     Ⓗ Daisy
     Ⓙ Tulip

Table of Contents
Math

Unit 1	Concepts	
Lesson		Page
❏ 1	Numeration	95
❏ 2	Number Concepts	97
❏ 3	Properties	99
❏ 4	Test Yourself	101

Unit 2	Computation	
Lesson		Page
❏ 5	Addition	104
❏ 6	Subtraction	106
❏ 7	Multiplication and Division	108
❏ 8	Test Yourself	110

Unit 3	Applications	
Lesson		Page
❏ 9	Geometry	113
❏ 10	Measurement	117
❏ 11	Problem Solving	121
❏ 12	Test Yourself	125
❏	Name and Answer Sheet	129

Unit 4	Test Practice	
Part		Page
❏ 1	Concepts	131
❏ 2	Computation	134
❏ 3	Applications	136

UNIT 1 CONCEPTS
Lesson 1 Numeration

Example **Directions:** Read and work each problem. Find the correct answer. Mark the space for your choice.

A Which of these is greater than 4?
- Ⓐ 2
- Ⓑ 3
- Ⓒ 4
- Ⓓ 5

B What is another name for 68?
- Ⓕ 8 tens and 6 ones
- Ⓖ 6 tens and 8 ones
- Ⓗ 7 tens and 8 ones
- Ⓙ 5 tens and 18 ones

Tips Read each question carefully. Look for key words and numbers that will help you find the answers.

Practice

1 What number goes in the box on this number line?

49 51   □   65

- Ⓐ 58
- Ⓑ 60
- Ⓒ 61
- Ⓓ 63

2 A group of students were recording the amount of rain that fell during each day in April. All their measurements were between 0.15 and 1.28 inches. Which of the measurements below might they have taken?

- Ⓕ 0.58
- Ⓖ 0.08
- Ⓗ 2.26
- Ⓙ 1.51

3 Your friend is twelfth in line for a roller coaster ride. Exactly how many people are ahead of your friend?

- Ⓐ 10
- Ⓑ 11
- Ⓒ 14
- Ⓓ 17

4 Which of these groups has five more bananas than monkeys?

GO

ANSWER ROWS   A Ⓐ Ⓑ Ⓒ Ⓓ   1 Ⓐ Ⓑ Ⓒ Ⓓ   3 Ⓐ Ⓑ Ⓒ Ⓓ
              B Ⓕ Ⓖ Ⓗ Ⓙ   2 Ⓕ Ⓖ Ⓗ Ⓙ   4 Ⓕ Ⓖ Ⓗ Ⓙ

95

5 Which of these shows numerals in the correct counting order?

- Ⓐ 27, 29, 38, 30
- Ⓑ 26, 27, 28, 29
- Ⓒ 25, 28, 29, 30
- Ⓓ 24, 23, 22, 21

6 How many of these numbers are greater than 128?

| 182 104 127 227 119 132 |

- Ⓕ 2
- Ⓖ 3
- Ⓗ 4
- Ⓙ 5

7 Another name for 4 hundreds, 7 tens and 9 ones is

- Ⓐ 479
- Ⓑ 40,079
- Ⓒ 4709
- Ⓓ 4791

8 The number 978 is less than

- Ⓕ 878
- Ⓖ 966
- Ⓗ 789
- Ⓙ 998

9 Which of these shows the same number of carrots and pears?

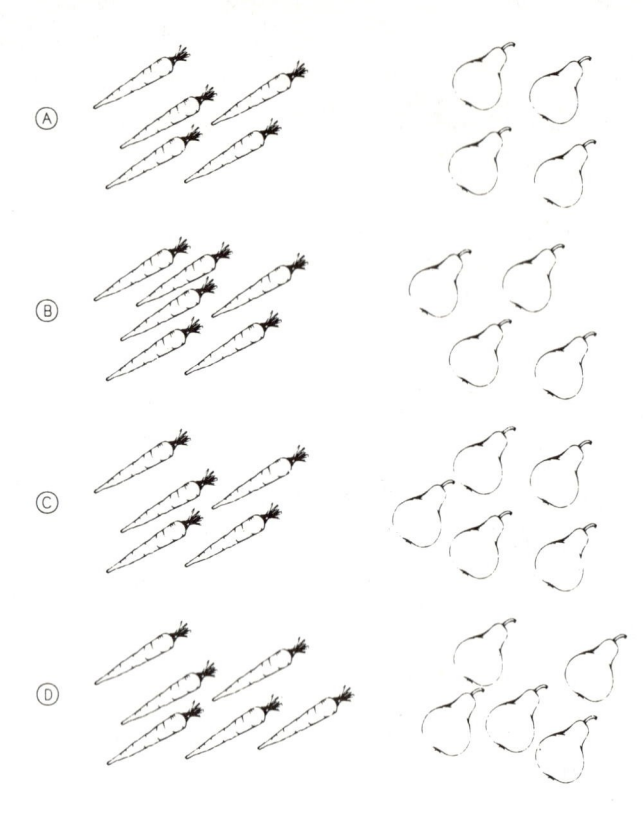

10 If you arranged these numbers from least to greatest, which would be last?

| 1038 1084 1308 1208 1803 |

- Ⓕ 1803
- Ⓖ 1208
- Ⓗ 1084
- Ⓙ 1308

11 How many tens are in 47?

- Ⓐ 47
- Ⓑ 10
- Ⓒ 7
- Ⓓ 4

Lesson 2   Number Concepts

Example   **Directions:** Read and work each problem. Find the correct answer. Mark the space for your choice.

A Which of these is fifty-seven?
- Ⓐ 50
- Ⓑ 57
- Ⓒ 75
- Ⓓ 507

B Which of these is an even number?
- Ⓕ 11
- Ⓖ 9
- Ⓗ 8
- Ⓙ 5

Tips

Key words, numbers, pictures, and figures will help you find the answers.

When you are not sure of an answer, take your best guess.

Practice

1 What number do you think is represented by this chart?

100's	10's	1's
/ / /	/ / / / /	/ / / / / / /

- Ⓐ 15
- Ⓑ 357
- Ⓒ 3570
- Ⓓ 30,507

2 What number is missing from the sequence below?

   7, 16, 25, 34, ____, 52

- Ⓕ 38
- Ⓖ 39
- Ⓗ 42
- Ⓙ 43

3 8 hundreds and 6 thousands =
- Ⓐ 8600
- Ⓑ 8606
- Ⓒ 6800
- Ⓓ 806

4 From the figures below, you know that

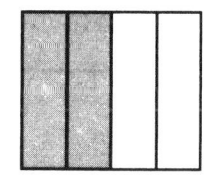

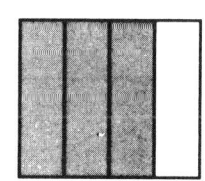

- Ⓕ $\frac{3}{4}$ is greater than $\frac{1}{2}$.
- Ⓖ $\frac{1}{3}$ is greater than $\frac{1}{2}$.
- Ⓗ $\frac{3}{4}$ is less than $\frac{1}{2}$.
- Ⓙ $\frac{3}{4}$ is less than $\frac{1}{3}$.

Lesson 2　Number Concepts

5 Counting by tens, which number comes after 50 and before 70?

- Ⓐ 60
- Ⓑ 80
- Ⓒ 90
- Ⓓ 160

6 Which of the numbers below has a 5 in the hundreds place?

- Ⓕ 2395
- Ⓖ 3259
- Ⓗ 5932
- Ⓙ 9532

7 Which group of numbers has three even numbers?

- Ⓐ 8, 9, 16, 20, 44, 90, 97
- Ⓑ 4, 9, 15, 27, 46, 68, 71
- Ⓒ 3, 21, 44, 66, 75, 83, 93
- Ⓓ 7, 24, 32, 56, 71, 82, 95

8 How much of this figure is shaded?

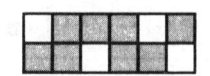

- Ⓕ $\frac{3}{4}$
- Ⓖ $\frac{2}{3}$
- Ⓗ $\frac{1}{3}$
- Ⓙ $\frac{3}{10}$

9 Which of these numbers is even and can be divided by 5?

- Ⓐ 58
- Ⓑ 21
- Ⓒ 15
- Ⓓ 10

10 Which of these fractions is the smallest?

- Ⓕ $\frac{1}{2}$
- Ⓖ $\frac{2}{3}$
- Ⓗ $\frac{1}{9}$
- Ⓙ $\frac{3}{4}$

11 Look at the pattern below. Which shape is missing from the pattern?

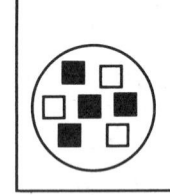

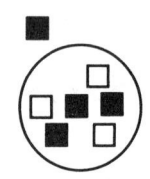

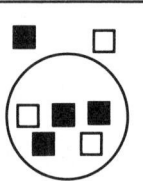

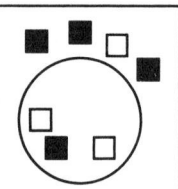

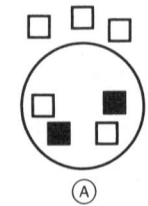

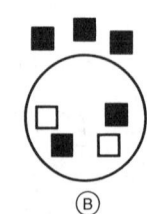

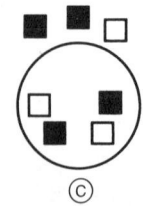

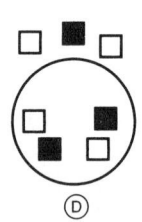

Lesson 3 Properties

Example **Directions:** Read and work each problem. Find the correct answer. Mark the space for your choice.

A What number completes the number sentence ☐ + 0 = 5?

- Ⓐ 0
- Ⓑ 5
- Ⓒ 10
- Ⓓ 50

B What is 285 rounded to the nearest hundred?

- Ⓕ 200
- Ⓖ 280
- Ⓗ 290
- Ⓙ 300

Tips

Read the question carefully. Think about what the question is asking before you choose an answer.

If you work on scratch paper, be sure you transfer numbers correctly.

Practice

1 What number completes both of the number sentences below?

$$21 - \square = 17$$
$$8 + \square = 12$$

- Ⓐ 4
- Ⓑ 5
- Ⓒ 9
- Ⓓ 13

2 Which of the number sentences below is true?

- Ⓕ 299 < 290
- Ⓖ 299 > 390
- Ⓗ 390 = 290
- Ⓙ 390 > 299

3 Which of these answer choices is closest in value to 140?

- Ⓐ 39
- Ⓑ 129
- Ⓒ 136
- Ⓓ 148

4 What symbol correctly completes the number sentence below?

$$7 \; \square \; 3 = 21$$

- Ⓕ ÷
- Ⓖ ×
- Ⓗ −
- Ⓙ +

GO

ANSWER ROWS A Ⓐ Ⓑ Ⓒ Ⓓ   1 Ⓐ Ⓑ Ⓒ Ⓓ   3 Ⓐ Ⓑ Ⓒ Ⓓ
            B Ⓕ Ⓖ Ⓗ Ⓙ   2 Ⓕ Ⓖ Ⓗ Ⓙ   4 Ⓕ Ⓖ Ⓗ Ⓙ

Lesson 3   Properties

5   Another way to write 3 x 7 is

  Ⓐ 7 x 3 x 3

  Ⓑ 3 + 7

  Ⓒ 7 x 7 x 7

  Ⓓ 7 + 7 + 7

6   If you round the numbers below to the nearest hundred, how many of them would be 300?

  321, 233, 402, 287, 430, 294

  Ⓕ 2

  Ⓖ 3

  Ⓗ 4

  Ⓙ 6

7 $\frac{1}{4} = \frac{3}{\square}$ $\square =$

  Ⓐ 3

  Ⓑ 6

  Ⓒ 12

  Ⓓ 24

8   0.7 =

  Ⓕ $\frac{7}{10}$

  Ⓖ $\frac{7}{100}$

  Ⓗ $\frac{7}{70}$

  Ⓙ $\frac{70}{10}$

9   What sign belongs in the circle in the number sentence below?

  10 − 1 = 7 ◯ 2

  Ⓐ −

  Ⓑ +

  Ⓒ x

  Ⓓ ÷

10   Suppose you wanted to estimate how to find 73 x 48 to the nearest 10. Which of these would you use?

  Ⓕ 100 x 40

  Ⓖ 100 x 50

  Ⓗ 70 x 50

  Ⓙ 70 x 40

11   Which number sentence shows how to find the total number of chairs in the box?

  3 + 5 = ☐   3 − 5 = ☐   3 x 5 = ☐   3 ÷ 5 = ☐
       Ⓐ   Ⓑ   Ⓒ   Ⓓ

ANSWER ROWS   5 Ⓐ Ⓑ Ⓒ Ⓓ   7 Ⓐ Ⓑ Ⓒ Ⓓ   9 Ⓐ Ⓑ Ⓒ Ⓓ   11 Ⓐ Ⓑ Ⓒ Ⓓ
100   6 Ⓕ Ⓖ Ⓗ Ⓙ   8 Ⓕ Ⓖ Ⓗ Ⓙ   10 Ⓕ Ⓖ Ⓗ Ⓙ

Lesson 4 Test Yourself

Examples Directions: Read and work each problem. Find the correct answer. Mark the space for your choice.

E1

Twenty apples were on a tree. Six fell off. How can you find the number left?

- Ⓐ add
- Ⓑ subtract
- Ⓒ multiply
- Ⓓ divide

E2

Which letter of the alphabet comes immediately after the tenth letter?

- Ⓕ J
- Ⓖ K
- Ⓗ M
- Ⓙ P

---

1 Which of these means three thousand, nine hundred forty-six?

- Ⓐ 3006
- Ⓑ 3046
- Ⓒ 3900
- Ⓓ 3946

2 Look at the counting pattern below. What number comes next?

| 429 | 433 | 437 | 441 | |

- Ⓕ 443
- Ⓖ 444
- Ⓗ 445
- Ⓙ 447

3 Which point on the number line below is closest to 7.1?

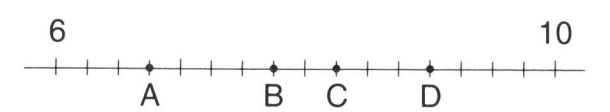

6   10
+-+-+-+-+-+-+-+-+-+-+
    A   B C   D

- Ⓐ A
- Ⓑ B
- Ⓒ C
- Ⓓ D

4 Counting by ones, what number comes before 249?

- Ⓕ 248
- Ⓖ 250
- Ⓗ 251
- Ⓙ 348

5 Which of these numbers has a 1 in the tens place and a 7 in the ones place?

- Ⓐ 710
- Ⓑ 701
- Ⓒ 517
- Ⓓ 471

6 If one more block in this figure were shaded, what fraction of the figure would be shaded?

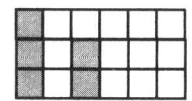

- Ⓕ $\frac{1}{6}$
- Ⓖ $\frac{1}{3}$
- Ⓗ $\frac{1}{2}$
- Ⓙ $\frac{2}{3}$

GO ▶

ANSWER ROWS   E1 Ⓐ Ⓑ Ⓒ Ⓓ   1 Ⓐ Ⓑ Ⓒ Ⓓ   3 Ⓐ Ⓑ Ⓒ Ⓓ   5 Ⓐ Ⓑ Ⓒ Ⓓ
              E2 Ⓕ Ⓖ Ⓗ Ⓙ   2 Ⓕ Ⓖ Ⓗ Ⓙ   4 Ⓕ Ⓖ Ⓗ Ⓙ   6 Ⓕ Ⓖ Ⓗ Ⓙ

7 Look at the number below. Suppose you increased the value of the digit in the hundreds place by 2. What would the new number be?

1429

- Ⓐ 3429
- Ⓑ 1449
- Ⓒ 1629
- Ⓓ 1431

8 What is 3,297,495 rounded to the nearest hundred thousand?

- Ⓕ 3,330,300
- Ⓖ 3,300,300
- Ⓗ 3,030,000
- Ⓙ 3,300,000

9 Which of these patterns shows counting by threes?

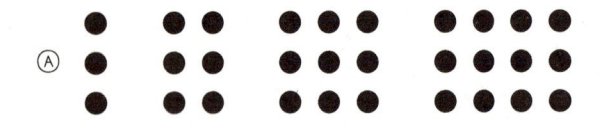

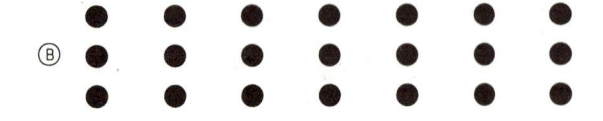

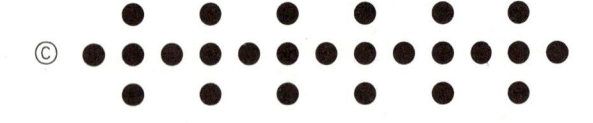

10 If you arranged these numbers from least to greatest, which would be in the middle?

934   199   560   237   248

- Ⓕ 237
- Ⓖ 248
- Ⓗ 199
- Ⓙ 560

11 Which of these is the same as $\frac{43}{100}$?

- Ⓐ 4.3
- Ⓑ 0.043
- Ⓒ 0.43
- Ⓓ 43

12 What should replace the □ in the number sentence below?

20 + □ = 20

- Ⓕ 0
- Ⓖ 1
- Ⓗ 20
- Ⓙ 100

13 In which of these must you rename a ten as ten ones or borrow a ten?

- Ⓐ 29 − 6 =
- Ⓑ 36 − 0 =
- Ⓒ 19 − 5 =
- Ⓓ 15 − 9 =

Lesson 4   Test Yourself

14 What should replace the circle in this multiplication problem?

$$\begin{array}{r} 41 \\ \times\ 2 \\ \hline \bigcirc 2 \end{array}$$

- Ⓕ 0
- Ⓖ 6
- Ⓗ 8
- Ⓙ 9

15 Counting by fours, what comes after 28?

- Ⓐ 32
- Ⓑ 30
- Ⓒ 24
- Ⓓ 8

16 Which of these shows a shaded area that is greater than one half?

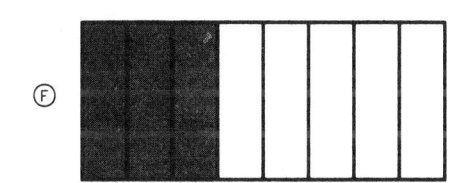

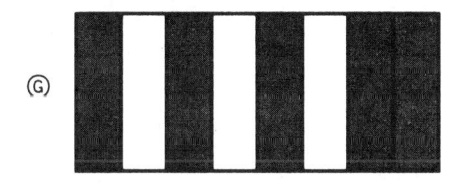

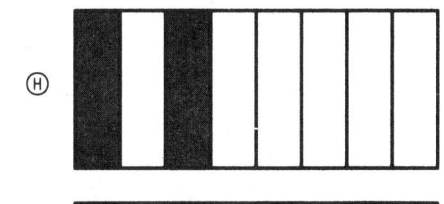

Ⓕ
Ⓖ
Ⓗ
Ⓙ

17 Which of these is greater than 35 and can be divided by 7?

- Ⓐ 14
- Ⓑ 35
- Ⓒ 41
- Ⓓ 42

18 Which number, if placed in both boxes, will make the number sentence below true?

$$8 + \Box + \Box = 30$$

- Ⓕ 9
- Ⓖ 11
- Ⓗ 22
- Ⓙ 38

19 Which numeral means thirty one thousand, fifty six?

- Ⓐ 310,056
- Ⓑ 31,560
- Ⓒ 31,056
- Ⓓ 30,156

20 Which of these is the best way to estimate the answer to this problem?

$$286 \times 109 = \Box$$

- Ⓕ 300 × 100 = □
- Ⓖ 200 × 100 = □
- Ⓗ 300 × 200 = □
- Ⓙ 100 × 100 = □

103

STOP

ANSWER ROWS   14 Ⓕ Ⓖ Ⓗ Ⓙ   16 Ⓕ Ⓖ Ⓗ Ⓙ   18 Ⓕ Ⓖ Ⓗ Ⓙ   20 Ⓕ Ⓖ Ⓗ Ⓙ
               15 Ⓐ Ⓑ Ⓒ Ⓓ   17 Ⓐ Ⓑ Ⓒ Ⓓ   19 Ⓐ Ⓑ Ⓒ Ⓓ

NUMBER RIGHT _____

UNIT 2 COMPUTATION

Lesson 5 Addition

Example **Directions:** Mark the space for the correct answer to each addition problem. Choose "None of these" if the right answer is not given.

A		B	
4 + 7	Ⓐ 3 Ⓑ 11 Ⓒ 12 Ⓓ 47 Ⓔ None of these	27 + 3 =	Ⓕ 20 Ⓖ 29 Ⓗ 32 Ⓙ 33 Ⓚ None of these

Tips

Be sure to add carefully.

If the right answer is not given, mark the space for "None of these."

Practice

1 26 + 6 =
Ⓐ 32
Ⓑ 31
Ⓒ 30
Ⓓ 20
Ⓔ None of these

2
1368
+ 5121
Ⓕ 5489
Ⓖ 6487
Ⓗ 6489
Ⓙ 6589
Ⓚ None of these

3 32 + 81 =
Ⓐ 111
Ⓑ 113
Ⓒ 123
Ⓓ 124
Ⓔ None of these

4
22
11
+ 43
Ⓕ 33
Ⓖ 54
Ⓗ 66
Ⓙ 76
Ⓚ None of these

5
841
+ 66
Ⓐ 807
Ⓑ 1007
Ⓒ 1447
Ⓓ 1507
Ⓔ None of these

6
402
+ 183
Ⓕ 585
Ⓖ 595
Ⓗ 603
Ⓙ 782
Ⓚ None of these

7
104
21
+ 52
Ⓐ 73
Ⓑ 156
Ⓒ 177
Ⓓ 357
Ⓔ None of these

8 14 + 19 + 4 =
Ⓕ 27
Ⓖ 37
Ⓗ 44
Ⓙ 73
Ⓚ None of these

GO

ANSWER ROWS A Ⓐ Ⓑ Ⓒ Ⓓ Ⓔ   1 Ⓐ Ⓑ Ⓒ Ⓓ Ⓔ   3 Ⓐ Ⓑ Ⓒ Ⓓ Ⓔ   5 Ⓐ Ⓑ Ⓒ Ⓓ Ⓔ   7 Ⓐ Ⓑ Ⓒ Ⓓ Ⓔ
             B Ⓕ Ⓖ Ⓗ Ⓙ Ⓚ   2 Ⓕ Ⓖ Ⓗ Ⓙ Ⓚ   4 Ⓕ Ⓖ Ⓗ Ⓙ Ⓚ   6 Ⓕ Ⓖ Ⓗ Ⓙ Ⓚ   8 Ⓕ Ⓖ Ⓗ Ⓙ Ⓚ

Lesson 5   Addition

9. $\frac{1}{7} + \frac{3}{7} =$
    - Ⓐ $\frac{2}{7}$
    - Ⓑ $\frac{4}{14}$
    - Ⓒ $\frac{3}{7}$
    - Ⓓ $\frac{4}{7}$
    - Ⓔ None of these

10. $41 + 29 + 7 + 2 =$
    - Ⓕ 70
    - Ⓖ 76
    - Ⓗ 78
    - Ⓙ 81
    - Ⓚ None of these

11. 700
    + 700
    - Ⓐ 770
    - Ⓑ 1400
    - Ⓒ 1700
    - Ⓓ 7700
    - Ⓔ None of these

12. 7288
    + 932
    - Ⓕ 8220
    - Ⓖ 7220
    - Ⓗ 6426
    - Ⓙ 6356
    - Ⓚ None of these

13. $6.37 + $5.94 =
    - Ⓐ $0.43
    - Ⓑ $11.23
    - Ⓒ $11.31
    - Ⓓ $12.31
    - Ⓔ None of these

14. 7.6
    + 0.25
    - Ⓕ 7.35
    - Ⓖ 7.41
    - Ⓗ 7.75
    - Ⓙ 7.85
    - Ⓚ None of these

15. $25 + 28 =$
    - Ⓐ 53
    - Ⓑ 54
    - Ⓒ 63
    - Ⓓ 107
    - Ⓔ None of these

16. 261
    17
    + 503
    - Ⓕ 520
    - Ⓖ 771
    - Ⓗ 776
    - Ⓙ 781
    - Ⓚ None of these

17. 489
    + 33
    - Ⓐ 512
    - Ⓑ 522
    - Ⓒ 532
    - Ⓓ 582
    - Ⓔ None of these

18. $2.7 + 4.8 =$
    - Ⓕ 2.1
    - Ⓖ 6.1
    - Ⓗ 6.5
    - Ⓙ 7.6
    - Ⓚ None of these

19. 80
    10
    + 30
    - Ⓐ 130
    - Ⓑ 120
    - Ⓒ 110
    - Ⓓ 93
    - Ⓔ None of these

20. 199
    + 222
    - Ⓕ 301
    - Ⓖ 311
    - Ⓗ 421
    - Ⓙ 422
    - Ⓚ None of these

STOP

ANSWER ROWS
9 Ⓐ Ⓑ Ⓒ Ⓓ Ⓔ   12 Ⓕ Ⓖ Ⓗ Ⓙ Ⓚ   15 Ⓐ Ⓑ Ⓒ Ⓓ Ⓔ   18 Ⓕ Ⓖ Ⓗ Ⓙ Ⓚ
10 Ⓕ Ⓖ Ⓗ Ⓙ Ⓚ   13 Ⓐ Ⓑ Ⓒ Ⓓ Ⓔ   16 Ⓕ Ⓖ Ⓗ Ⓙ Ⓚ   19 Ⓐ Ⓑ Ⓒ Ⓓ Ⓔ
11 Ⓐ Ⓑ Ⓒ Ⓓ Ⓔ   14 Ⓕ Ⓖ Ⓗ Ⓙ Ⓚ   17 Ⓐ Ⓑ Ⓒ Ⓓ Ⓔ   20 Ⓕ Ⓖ Ⓗ Ⓙ Ⓚ

Lesson 6 Subtraction

Example

Directions: Mark the space for the correct answer to each subtraction problem. Choose "NG" if the right answer is not given.

A

13 − 8 =

- Ⓐ 3
- Ⓑ 4
- Ⓒ 5
- Ⓓ 21
- Ⓔ NG

B

9
− 3

- Ⓕ 5
- Ⓖ 7
- Ⓗ 11
- Ⓙ 12
- Ⓚ NG

Tips

If the right answer is not given, mark the space for "NG." This means "not given."

When you are not sure of an answer, check it by adding.

Practice

1

27
− 4

- Ⓐ 13
- Ⓑ 23
- Ⓒ 27
- Ⓓ 31
- Ⓔ NG

5

200 − 60 =

- Ⓐ 260
- Ⓑ 240
- Ⓒ 144
- Ⓓ 140
- Ⓔ NG

2

59
− 17

- Ⓕ 32
- Ⓖ 43
- Ⓗ 62
- Ⓙ 76
- Ⓚ NG

6

6.78
− 0.6

- Ⓕ 6.18
- Ⓖ 5.72
- Ⓗ 5.18
- Ⓙ 0.78
- Ⓚ NG

3

42
− 19

- Ⓐ 61
- Ⓑ 51
- Ⓒ 33
- Ⓓ 23
- Ⓔ NG

7

795
− 83

- Ⓐ 612
- Ⓑ 711
- Ⓒ 718
- Ⓓ 878
- Ⓔ NG

4

96 − 48 =

- Ⓕ 48
- Ⓖ 49
- Ⓗ 54
- Ⓙ 58
- Ⓚ NG

8

129
− 51

- Ⓕ 68
- Ⓖ 78
- Ⓗ 138
- Ⓙ 180
- Ⓚ NG

GO

ANSWER ROWS A Ⓐ Ⓑ Ⓒ Ⓓ Ⓔ   1 Ⓐ Ⓑ Ⓒ Ⓓ Ⓔ   3 Ⓐ Ⓑ Ⓒ Ⓓ Ⓔ   5 Ⓐ Ⓑ Ⓒ Ⓓ Ⓔ   7 Ⓐ Ⓑ Ⓒ Ⓓ Ⓔ
             B Ⓕ Ⓖ Ⓗ Ⓙ Ⓚ   2 Ⓕ Ⓖ Ⓗ Ⓙ Ⓚ   4 Ⓕ Ⓖ Ⓗ Ⓙ Ⓚ   6 Ⓕ Ⓖ Ⓗ Ⓙ Ⓚ   8 Ⓕ Ⓖ Ⓗ Ⓙ Ⓚ

Lesson 6　Subtraction

9　$0.82 − $0.24 =
- (A) $0.40
- (B) $0.52
- (C) $0.58
- (D) $1.06
- (E) NG

10
$$\begin{array}{r}418\\-232\\\hline\end{array}$$
- (F) 114
- (G) 176
- (H) 186
- (J) 226
- (K) NG

11
$$\begin{array}{r}52\\-27\\\hline\end{array}$$
- (A) 25
- (B) 32
- (C) 35
- (D) 37
- (E) NG

12　$\frac{8}{9} - \frac{4}{9} =$
- (F) $\frac{5}{18}$
- (G) $\frac{4}{9}$
- (H) $\frac{5}{9}$
- (J) 5
- (K) NG

13
$$\begin{array}{r}8686\\-275\\\hline\end{array}$$
- (A) 8411
- (B) 8409
- (C) 8301
- (D) 7411
- (E) NG

14
$$\begin{array}{r}6009\\-3115\\\hline\end{array}$$
- (F) 2814
- (G) 2893
- (H) 3894
- (J) 3994
- (K) NG

15　66 − 3 =
- (A) 36
- (B) 52
- (C) 59
- (D) 63
- (E) NG

16
$$\begin{array}{r}70\\-20\\\hline\end{array}$$
- (F) 40
- (G) 48
- (H) 68
- (J) 90
- (K) NG

17　48 − 29 =
- (A) 27
- (B) 21
- (C) 19
- (D) 17
- (E) NG

18
$$\begin{array}{r}\$6.25\\-\$0.11\\\hline\end{array}$$
- (F) $5.11
- (G) $5.14
- (H) $6.04
- (J) $6.14
- (K) NG

19
$$\begin{array}{r}1000\\-275\\\hline\end{array}$$
- (A) 725
- (B) 775
- (C) 825
- (D) 875
- (E) NG

20
$$\begin{array}{r}400\\-131\\\hline\end{array}$$
- (F) 259
- (G) 269
- (H) 369
- (J) 331
- (K) NG

ANSWER ROWS
9 Ⓐ Ⓑ Ⓒ Ⓓ Ⓔ　12 Ⓕ Ⓖ Ⓗ Ⓙ Ⓚ　15 Ⓐ Ⓑ Ⓒ Ⓓ Ⓔ　18 Ⓕ Ⓖ Ⓗ Ⓙ Ⓚ
10 Ⓕ Ⓖ Ⓗ Ⓙ Ⓚ　13 Ⓐ Ⓑ Ⓒ Ⓓ Ⓔ　16 Ⓕ Ⓖ Ⓗ Ⓙ Ⓚ　19 Ⓐ Ⓑ Ⓒ Ⓓ Ⓔ
11 Ⓐ Ⓑ Ⓒ Ⓓ Ⓔ　14 Ⓕ Ⓖ Ⓗ Ⓙ Ⓚ　17 Ⓐ Ⓑ Ⓒ Ⓓ Ⓔ　20 Ⓕ Ⓖ Ⓗ Ⓙ Ⓚ

Lesson 7 Multiplication and Division

Example **Directions:** Mark the space for the correct answer to each multiplication or division problem. Choose "NH" if the right answer is not given.

A
$$\begin{array}{r} 7 \\ \times\ 6 \\ \hline \end{array}$$
- Ⓐ 13
- Ⓑ 24
- Ⓒ 40
- Ⓓ 42
- Ⓔ NH

B
$8 \div 2 =$
- Ⓕ 28
- Ⓖ 16
- Ⓗ 6
- Ⓙ 2
- Ⓚ NH

Tips

Pay careful attention to each problem so you perform the correct operation.

If the right answer is not given, mark the space for "NH." This means "not here."

Practice

1. $0 \times 4 =$
   - Ⓐ 44
   - Ⓑ 40
   - Ⓒ 4
   - Ⓓ 0
   - Ⓔ NH

5. $7 \times 7 =$
   - Ⓐ 49
   - Ⓑ 48
   - Ⓒ 39
   - Ⓓ 14
   - Ⓔ NH

2. $3\overline{)10}$
   - Ⓕ 3
   - Ⓖ 3 R1
   - Ⓗ 3 R2
   - Ⓙ 4
   - Ⓚ NH

6. $\begin{array}{r} 310 \\ \times\ 5 \\ \hline \end{array}$
   - Ⓕ 1650
   - Ⓖ 1550
   - Ⓗ 315
   - Ⓙ 305
   - Ⓚ NH

3. $\begin{array}{r} 44 \\ \times\ 4 \\ \hline \end{array}$
   - Ⓐ 48
   - Ⓑ 166
   - Ⓒ 176
   - Ⓓ 256
   - Ⓔ NH

7. $2515 \div 5 =$
   - Ⓐ 623
   - Ⓑ 515
   - Ⓒ 512
   - Ⓓ 502
   - Ⓔ NH

4. $4\overline{)56}$
   - Ⓕ 12
   - Ⓖ 12 R2
   - Ⓗ 13 R3
   - Ⓙ 14
   - Ⓚ NH

8. $18 \div 3 = \square$
   - Ⓕ 15
   - Ⓖ 9
   - Ⓗ 8
   - Ⓙ 6
   - Ⓚ NH

GO

ANSWER ROWS 108
A Ⓐ Ⓑ Ⓒ Ⓓ Ⓔ   1 Ⓐ Ⓑ Ⓒ Ⓓ Ⓔ   3 Ⓐ Ⓑ Ⓒ Ⓓ Ⓔ   5 Ⓐ Ⓑ Ⓒ Ⓓ Ⓔ   7 Ⓐ Ⓑ Ⓒ Ⓓ Ⓔ
B Ⓕ Ⓖ Ⓗ Ⓙ Ⓚ   2 Ⓕ Ⓖ Ⓗ Ⓙ Ⓚ   4 Ⓕ Ⓖ Ⓗ Ⓙ Ⓚ   6 Ⓕ Ⓖ Ⓗ Ⓙ Ⓚ   8 Ⓕ Ⓖ Ⓗ Ⓙ Ⓚ

Lesson 7   Multiplication and Division

9

$4\overline{)800}$

- Ⓐ 20
- Ⓑ 80
- Ⓒ 100
- Ⓓ 200
- Ⓔ NH

15

$\begin{array}{r}28\\\times\ 3\\\hline\end{array}$

- Ⓐ 31
- Ⓑ 84
- Ⓒ 88
- Ⓓ 103
- Ⓔ NH

10

$7 \div 7 =$

- Ⓕ 1
- Ⓖ 2
- Ⓗ 11
- Ⓙ 49
- Ⓚ NH

16

$6\overline{)64}$

- Ⓕ 1 R4
- Ⓖ 10 R4
- Ⓗ 11
- Ⓙ 11 R2
- Ⓚ NH

11

$\begin{array}{r}212\\\times\ 26\\\hline\end{array}$

- Ⓐ 5422
- Ⓑ 5512
- Ⓒ 5522
- Ⓓ 5626
- Ⓔ NH

17

$\begin{array}{r}12\\\times\ 12\\\hline\end{array}$

- Ⓐ 104
- Ⓑ 112
- Ⓒ 122
- Ⓓ 144
- Ⓔ NH

12

$28 \div 4 =$

- Ⓕ 5
- Ⓖ 6
- Ⓗ 7
- Ⓙ 9
- Ⓚ NH

18

$7\overline{)49}$

- Ⓕ 4
- Ⓖ 5
- Ⓗ 6
- Ⓙ 8
- Ⓚ NH

13

$\begin{array}{r}4\\\times\ 2\\\hline\end{array}$

- Ⓐ 4
- Ⓑ 6
- Ⓒ 8
- Ⓓ 42
- Ⓔ NH

19 In the table below, the numbers in Column II are 4 times larger than those in Column I. Which number belongs in the empty space in the table?

Column I	Column II
2	8
3	12
4	

- Ⓐ 1
- Ⓑ 8
- Ⓒ 14
- Ⓓ 16
- Ⓔ NH

14

$8\overline{)0}$

- Ⓕ 0
- Ⓖ 6
- Ⓗ 8
- Ⓙ 10
- Ⓚ NH

STOP

109

Lesson 8 Test Yourself

Examples Directions: Read and work each problem. Mark the space for the correct answer. Choose "N" if the right answer is not given.

E1 12 + 3 =
- Ⓐ 16
- Ⓑ 15
- Ⓒ 11
- Ⓓ 9
- Ⓔ N

E2 3 × 0 =
- Ⓕ 1
- Ⓖ 3
- Ⓗ 4
- Ⓙ 30
- Ⓚ N

1 44 − 8 =
- Ⓐ 52
- Ⓑ 26
- Ⓒ 24
- Ⓓ 22
- Ⓔ N

6 764 − 283
- Ⓕ 947
- Ⓖ 581
- Ⓗ 521
- Ⓙ 481
- Ⓚ N

2 86 + 10
- Ⓕ 76
- Ⓖ 86
- Ⓗ 96
- Ⓙ 97
- Ⓚ N

7 6) 13
- Ⓐ 3
- Ⓑ 2 R3
- Ⓒ 2 R1
- Ⓓ 2
- Ⓔ N

3 9 × 5 =
- Ⓐ 45
- Ⓑ 48
- Ⓒ 59
- Ⓓ 63
- Ⓔ N

8 22 + 84 + 77
- Ⓕ 106
- Ⓖ 161
- Ⓗ 173
- Ⓙ 183
- Ⓚ N

4 $6.00 − $4.49 =
- Ⓕ $2.51
- Ⓖ $1.51
- Ⓗ $1.49
- Ⓙ $1.41
- Ⓚ N

9 903 − 77
- Ⓐ 974
- Ⓑ 926
- Ⓒ 874
- Ⓓ 816
- Ⓔ N

5 6 × 400 =
- Ⓐ 2600
- Ⓑ 2400
- Ⓒ 2200
- Ⓓ 2000
- Ⓔ N

10 7.8 + 4.1 =
- Ⓕ 11.9
- Ⓖ 11.81
- Ⓗ 11.18
- Ⓙ 10.9
- Ⓚ N

GO

Lesson 8　Test Yourself

11

$\frac{4}{5} - \frac{1}{5} =$

Ⓐ $\frac{1}{4}$
Ⓑ $\frac{3}{10}$
Ⓒ $\frac{3}{5}$
Ⓓ 3
Ⓔ N

12

$\begin{array}{r} 230 \\ \times 4 \\ \hline \end{array}$

Ⓕ 920
Ⓖ 824
Ⓗ 820
Ⓙ 724
Ⓚ N

13

$\begin{array}{r} 1.8 \\ + 0.89 \\ \hline \end{array}$

Ⓐ 1.89
Ⓑ 1.97
Ⓒ 2.09
Ⓓ 2.89
Ⓔ N

14

$\$0.68 + \$0.41 =$

Ⓕ $0.27
Ⓖ $0.69
Ⓗ $0.72
Ⓙ $1.09
Ⓚ N

15

$3 \times 61 =$

Ⓐ 318
Ⓑ 193
Ⓒ 183
Ⓓ 123
Ⓔ N

16

$12 \div 3 = \square$

Ⓕ 2
Ⓖ 3
Ⓗ 4
Ⓙ 9
Ⓚ N

17

$\begin{array}{r} 834 \\ - 699 \\ \hline \end{array}$

Ⓐ 134
Ⓑ 135
Ⓒ 265
Ⓓ 335
Ⓔ N

18

$51 + 24 + 9 + 8 =$

Ⓕ 75
Ⓖ 84
Ⓗ 92
Ⓙ 102
Ⓚ N

19

$96 - 30 =$

Ⓐ 36
Ⓑ 63
Ⓒ 93
Ⓓ 126
Ⓔ N

20

$\begin{array}{r} 6945 \\ + 6336 \\ \hline \end{array}$

Ⓕ 13,281
Ⓖ 13,271
Ⓗ 12,881
Ⓙ 12,281
Ⓚ N

21

$\begin{array}{r} 802 \\ \times 11 \\ \hline \end{array}$

Ⓐ 809
Ⓑ 813
Ⓒ 8082
Ⓓ 8822
Ⓔ N

22

$\begin{array}{r} \$4.99 \\ - 3.29 \\ \hline \end{array}$

Ⓕ $1.67
Ⓖ $1.70
Ⓗ $1.90
Ⓙ $1.99
Ⓚ N

GO

ANSWER ROWS
11 Ⓐ Ⓑ Ⓒ Ⓓ Ⓔ　14 Ⓕ Ⓖ Ⓗ Ⓙ Ⓚ　17 Ⓐ Ⓑ Ⓒ Ⓓ Ⓔ　20 Ⓕ Ⓖ Ⓗ Ⓙ Ⓚ
12 Ⓕ Ⓖ Ⓗ Ⓙ Ⓚ　15 Ⓐ Ⓑ Ⓒ Ⓓ Ⓔ　18 Ⓕ Ⓖ Ⓗ Ⓙ Ⓚ　21 Ⓐ Ⓑ Ⓒ Ⓓ Ⓔ
13 Ⓐ Ⓑ Ⓒ Ⓓ Ⓔ　16 Ⓕ Ⓖ Ⓗ Ⓙ Ⓚ　19 Ⓐ Ⓑ Ⓒ Ⓓ Ⓔ　22 Ⓕ Ⓖ Ⓗ Ⓙ Ⓚ

Lesson 8   Test Yourself

23. $\frac{1}{3} + \frac{1}{3} =$
    - Ⓐ $\frac{1}{9}$
    - Ⓑ $\frac{1}{3}$
    - Ⓒ $\frac{2}{3}$
    - Ⓓ 1
    - Ⓔ N

24. $3 \times 93 =$
    - Ⓕ 249
    - Ⓖ 267
    - Ⓗ 273
    - Ⓙ 279
    - Ⓚ N

25. $4 + 7 + 6 =$
    - Ⓐ 13
    - Ⓑ 17
    - Ⓒ 19
    - Ⓓ 29
    - Ⓔ N

26. $4\overline{)80}$
    - Ⓕ 32
    - Ⓖ 30
    - Ⓗ 20 R4
    - Ⓙ 20
    - Ⓚ N

27. 124
    62
    + 477
    - Ⓐ 549
    - Ⓑ 562
    - Ⓒ 563
    - Ⓓ 653
    - Ⓔ N

28. $7\overline{)3654}$
    - Ⓕ 622
    - Ⓖ 522
    - Ⓗ 521
    - Ⓙ 489
    - Ⓚ N

29. $15 + 22 =$
    - Ⓐ 7
    - Ⓑ 32
    - Ⓒ 37
    - Ⓓ 172
    - Ⓔ N

30. $\$1.25 - \$1.19 =$
    - Ⓕ $1.44
    - Ⓖ $1.34
    - Ⓗ $0.16
    - Ⓙ $0.06
    - Ⓚ N

31. 40
    × 11
    - Ⓐ 440
    - Ⓑ 411
    - Ⓒ 410
    - Ⓓ 51
    - Ⓔ N

32. $100 \div 10 =$
    - Ⓕ 101
    - Ⓖ 11
    - Ⓗ 1
    - Ⓙ 0
    - Ⓚ N

33. In the table below, the numbers in Column II are 7 times larger than those in Column I. Which numbers belong in the empty spaces in the table?

Column I	Column II
3	21
4	
5	35
6	

- Ⓐ 14, 21
- Ⓑ 21, 35
- Ⓒ 27, 43
- Ⓓ 28, 42
- Ⓔ N

UNIT 3   Applications

Lesson 9   Geometry

Example   **Directions:** Find the correct answer to each geometry problem. Mark the space for your choice.

A What is the area of the shape on the right?

- Ⓐ 4 square units
- Ⓑ 5 square units
- Ⓒ 7 square units
- Ⓓ 8 square units

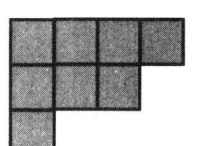

Tips

Pay careful attention to key words, numbers, pictures, and figures. They will help you find the answers.

When you are not sure of an answer, eliminate the choices you know are wrong, then take your best guess.

Practice

1 Which of these letters can be folded in half so the parts match exactly?

- Ⓐ J
- Ⓑ F
- Ⓒ H
- Ⓓ L

2 Look at the shapes below. Which one comes on the left of the largest square?

- Ⓕ the smallest circle
- Ⓖ the largest square
- Ⓗ the smallest square
- Ⓙ the medium-sized circle

3 This shape is called a —

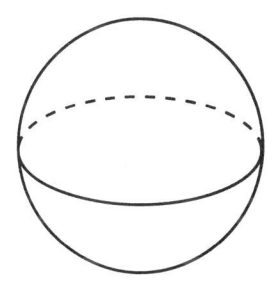

- Ⓐ cube
- Ⓑ sphere
- Ⓒ cylinder
- Ⓓ pyramid

4 A three-sided figure is a

- Ⓕ rectangle
- Ⓖ square
- Ⓗ circle
- Ⓙ triangle

GO

ANSWER ROWS   A Ⓐ Ⓑ Ⓒ Ⓓ   2 Ⓕ Ⓖ Ⓗ Ⓙ   4 Ⓕ Ⓖ Ⓗ Ⓙ
              1 Ⓐ Ⓑ Ⓒ Ⓓ   3 Ⓐ Ⓑ Ⓒ Ⓓ

Lesson 9   Geometry

5 Which of these shapes are congruent?

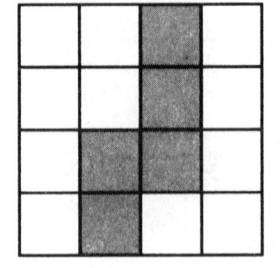

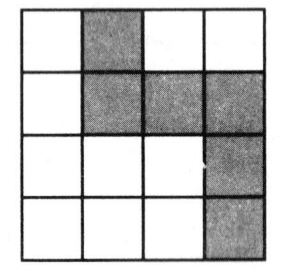

P

Q

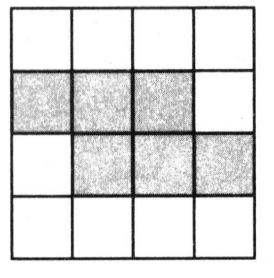

R

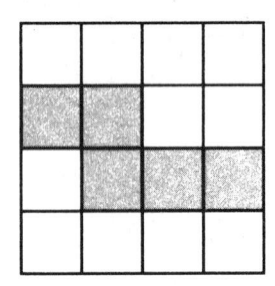

S

Ⓐ P, R, and S
Ⓑ P and S
Ⓒ Q and R
Ⓓ Q and S

6 Which of these figures has no line segments?

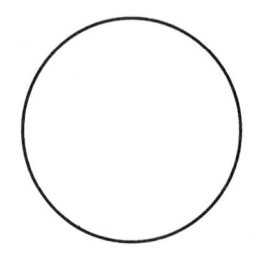

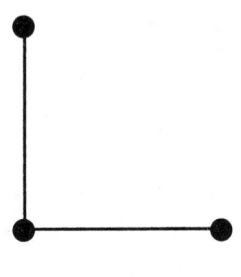

Ⓕ Ⓖ Ⓗ Ⓙ

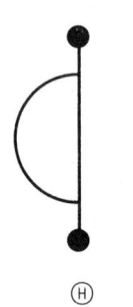

7 The perimeter of this shape is

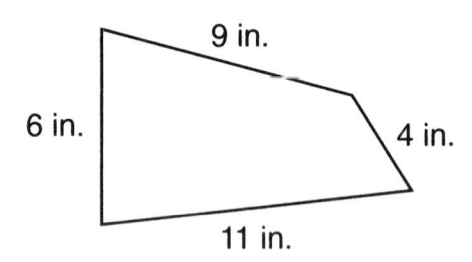

9 in.
6 in.
4 in.
11 in.

Ⓐ 10 in.
Ⓑ 20 in.
Ⓒ 29 in.
Ⓓ 30 in.

8 Congruent figures have

Ⓕ the same shape but different size
Ⓖ the same size but different shape
Ⓗ the same size and shape
Ⓙ different size and shape

114

ANSWER ROWS   5 Ⓐ Ⓑ Ⓒ Ⓓ   6 Ⓕ Ⓖ Ⓗ Ⓙ   7 Ⓐ Ⓑ Ⓒ Ⓓ   8 Ⓕ Ⓖ Ⓗ Ⓙ

GO

Lesson 9 Geometry

9 Which pair of figures has the same shape but different size?

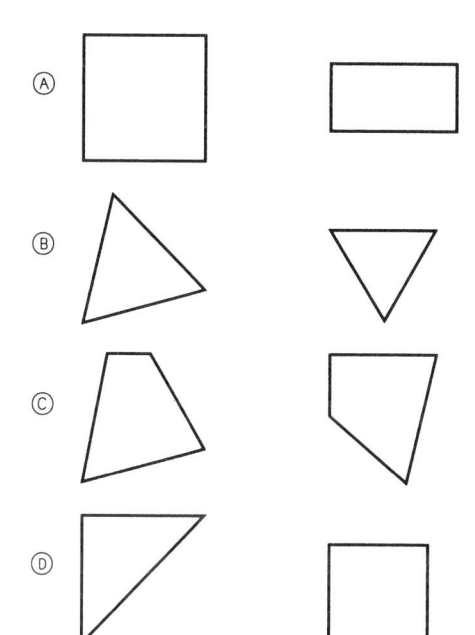

Ⓐ
Ⓑ
Ⓒ
Ⓓ

10 The perimeter of this figure is 32 units. How long is the missing side?

12 units
4 units   4 units
?

Ⓕ 12 units
Ⓖ 16 units
Ⓗ 24 units
Ⓙ 30 units

11 The area of the shaded portion of this shape is —

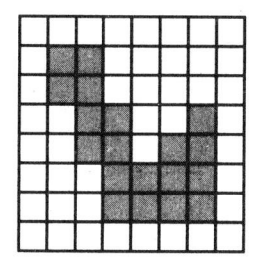

Ⓐ 64 sq. in.
Ⓑ 48 sq. in.
Ⓒ 19 sq. in.
Ⓓ 28 sq. in.

12 Which statement is true about the figure below?

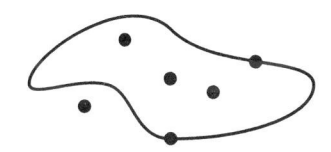

Ⓕ One dot is on the closed curve.
Ⓖ Three dots are inside the closed curve.
Ⓗ Three dots are on the closed curve.
Ⓙ Two dots are outside the closed curve.

13 Which of these figures is divided into three triangles?

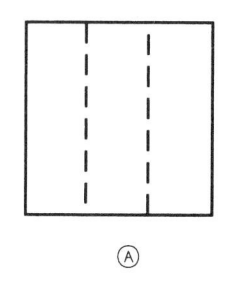

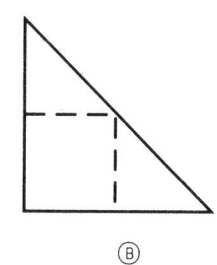

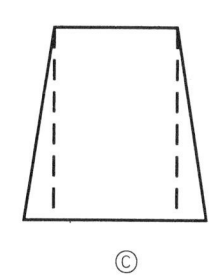

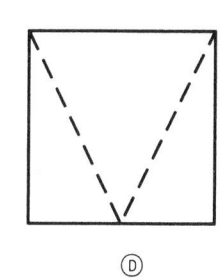

Ⓐ   Ⓑ   Ⓒ   Ⓓ

GO

ANSWER ROWS   9 Ⓐ Ⓑ Ⓒ Ⓓ   10 Ⓕ Ⓖ Ⓗ Ⓙ   11 Ⓐ Ⓑ Ⓒ Ⓓ   12 Ⓕ Ⓖ Ⓗ Ⓙ   13 Ⓐ Ⓑ Ⓒ Ⓓ | 115 |

Lesson 9   Geometry

14 If you cut a sphere in half any way, which of these would be formed?

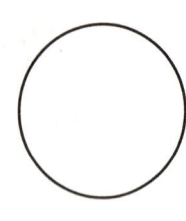

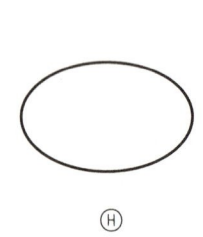

- F (square)
- G (circle)
- H (oval)
- J (rectangle)

15 A can is shaped like a
- Ⓐ sphere
- Ⓑ cube
- Ⓒ cone
- Ⓓ cylinder

16 The perimeter of this figure is

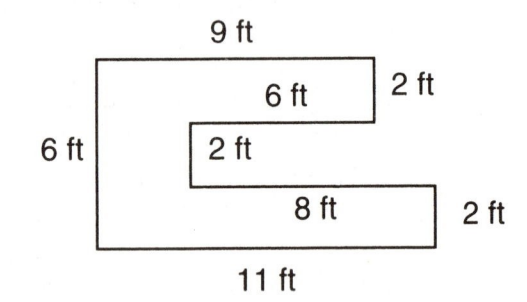

9 ft
6 ft
2 ft
6 ft
2 ft
8 ft
2 ft
11 ft

- F 46 ft
- G 42 ft
- H 40 ft
- J different size and shape

17 I have one more side than a triangle. All of my sides are equal. I am a —
- Ⓐ pyramid
- Ⓑ circle
- Ⓒ square
- Ⓓ triangle

18 One of these figures is not congruent with the others. Which one is it?

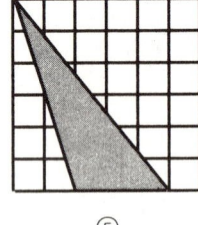

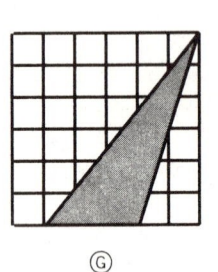

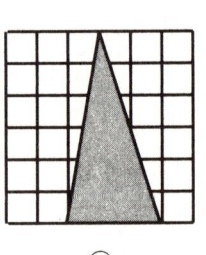

19 How would you find the area of the unshaded portion of this figure?

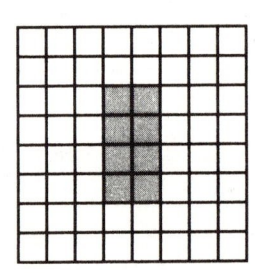

- Ⓐ 2 x 4
- Ⓑ 64 – 8
- Ⓒ 64 + 8
- Ⓓ 8 + 8 + 8 + 8

STOP

ANSWER ROWS 14 Ⓕ Ⓖ Ⓗ Ⓙ   16 Ⓕ Ⓖ Ⓗ Ⓙ   18 Ⓕ Ⓖ Ⓗ Ⓙ
15 Ⓐ Ⓑ Ⓒ Ⓓ   17 Ⓐ Ⓑ Ⓒ Ⓓ   19 Ⓐ Ⓑ Ⓒ Ⓓ

Lesson 10 Measurement

Example **Directions:** Find the correct answer to each measurement problem. Mark the space for your choice.

A What is the temperature shown on this thermometer?
- Ⓐ 18°
- Ⓑ 19°
- Ⓒ 21°
- Ⓓ 29°

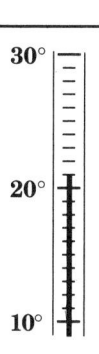

Tips: Read each question carefully. You can answer some questions without computing. If you must compute an answer, use scratch paper and work carefully.

Practice

1 Which of these statements is true?
- Ⓐ 1 foot = 21 inches
- Ⓑ 1 foot = 3 inches
- Ⓒ 1 yard = 36 inches
- Ⓓ 1 yard = 39 inches

2 A student bought a pen and received the coins below as change. The pen cost $1.25. How much money did the student give the cashier?

- Ⓕ $1.50
- Ⓖ $1.25
- Ⓗ $1.00
- Ⓙ $.25

3 A piece of typing paper is $8\frac{1}{2}$ by 11 inches. If you wanted to measure a piece of typing paper using the metric system, which unit would make the most sense?
- Ⓐ meters
- Ⓑ centimeters
- Ⓒ grams
- Ⓓ liters

4 It takes a train 36 hours to travel from Boston to Denver. This is the same as —
- Ⓕ half a day
- Ⓖ a day
- Ⓗ a day and a half
- Ⓙ two days

ANSWER ROWS A Ⓐ Ⓑ Ⓒ Ⓓ   2 Ⓕ Ⓖ Ⓗ Ⓙ   4 Ⓕ Ⓖ Ⓗ Ⓙ
1 Ⓐ Ⓑ Ⓒ Ⓓ   3 Ⓐ Ⓑ Ⓒ Ⓓ

Lesson 10   Measurement

5   What time is shown on this clock?

- Ⓐ 4:05
- Ⓑ 1:20
- Ⓒ 1:40
- Ⓓ 4:01

6   Milly looked at her watch and saw it was 10:40. Her next class begins in 25 minutes. What time does her next class begin?

- Ⓕ 10:55
- Ⓖ 11:20
- Ⓗ 11:05
- Ⓙ 10:45

7   Which of these is 1000 meters?

- Ⓐ a kilometer
- Ⓑ 0.01 kilometers
- Ⓒ a centimeter
- Ⓓ 100 centimeters

8   Which answer is the same as $6.28?

- Ⓕ six dollar bills, two dimes, three cents
- Ⓖ six dollar bills, a quarter, three cents
- Ⓗ five dollar bills, five quarters
- Ⓙ five dollar bills, five quarters, a dime

Use this calendar to answer questions 9 through 11.

SEPTEMBER						
SUN	MON	TUE	WED	THU	FRI	SAT
				1	2	3
4	5	6	7	8	9	10
11	12	13	14	15	16	17
18	19	20	21	22	23	24
25	26	27	28	29	30	

9   What date is the last Sunday of the month?

- Ⓐ September 25
- Ⓑ September 31
- Ⓒ September 18
- Ⓓ September 26

10   What day of the week is September 9?

- Ⓕ Wednesday
- Ⓖ Thursday
- Ⓗ Friday
- Ⓙ Monday

11   On Tuesday, September 13, the students in a class were given a homework assignment that was due the following Monday. What date was the homework assignment due?

- Ⓐ September 5
- Ⓑ September 13
- Ⓒ September 12
- Ⓓ September 19

Lesson 10   Measurement

12 About how long is this nail?

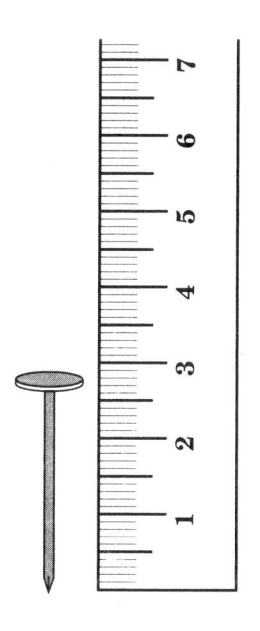

- ⓕ 1 cm
- ⓖ 3 cm
- ⓗ 4 cm
- ⓙ 6 cm

13 This thermometer shows the temperature at 8:00 in the morning. By noon, the temperature has risen by 12°. What is the temperature at noon?

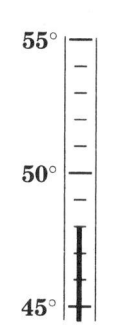

- Ⓐ 48°
- Ⓑ 58°
- Ⓒ 60°
- Ⓓ 92°

14 What time is shown on this clock?

- ⓕ 9:45
- ⓖ 8:50
- ⓗ 9:10
- ⓙ 9:50

15 A motorist crossed a bridge that has a toll of $1.50. The motorist paid the toll with a five-dollar bill. How much change did the motorist receive?

- Ⓐ $1.50
- Ⓑ $3.00
- Ⓒ $3.50
- Ⓓ $4.50

16 A group of students wants to weigh boxes of cereal to determine if the boxes contain as much cereal as they are supposed to. What unit of measure should the students use to get the most accurate measurement?

- ⓕ centimeters
- ⓖ pounds
- ⓗ kilograms
- ⓙ ounces

GO

ANSWER ROWS   12 ⓕⓖⓗⓙ   14 ⓕⓖⓗⓙ   16 ⓕⓖⓗⓙ
             13 ⒶⒷⒸⒹ   15 ⒶⒷⒸⒹ

119

Lesson 10   Measurement

17 What is the diameter of the circle shown below?

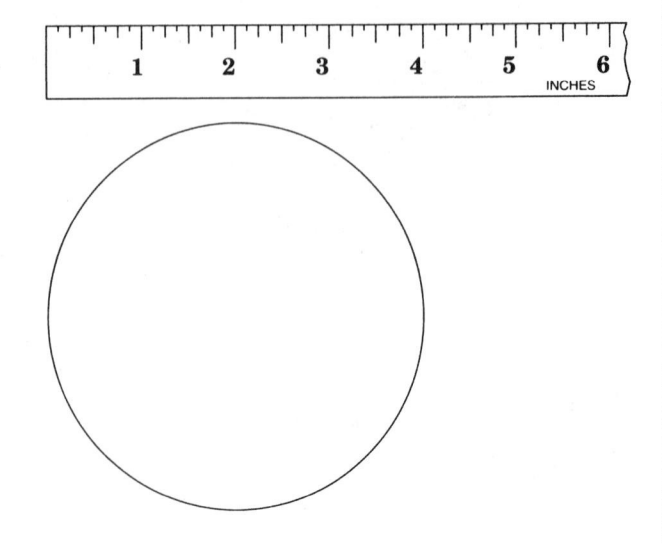

- Ⓐ 1 inch
- Ⓑ 2 inches
- Ⓒ 4 inches
- Ⓓ 6 inches

18 Which unit of measurement is longer than a foot but shorter than a meter?

- Ⓕ a yard
- Ⓖ a meter
- Ⓗ a centimeter
- Ⓙ a mile

19 On a summer day, you would feel most comfortable at what temperature?

- Ⓐ 35° F
- Ⓑ 30° F
- Ⓒ 95° F
- Ⓓ 75° F

20 Which of these clocks shows 5:20?

Ⓕ   Ⓖ   Ⓗ   Ⓙ

21 Look at the calendar below. What is the date of the second Sunday of March?

	March					
SUN	MON	TUE	WED	THU	FRI	SAT
	1	2	3	4	5	6
7	8	9	10	11	12	13
14	15	16	17	18	19	20
21	22	23	24	25	26	27
28	29	30	31			

- Ⓐ March 7
- Ⓑ March 14
- Ⓒ March 15
- Ⓓ March 13

STOP

ANSWER ROWS   17 Ⓐ Ⓑ Ⓒ Ⓓ   19 Ⓐ Ⓑ Ⓒ Ⓓ   21 Ⓐ Ⓑ Ⓒ Ⓓ
120   18 Ⓕ Ⓖ Ⓗ Ⓙ   20 Ⓕ Ⓖ Ⓗ Ⓙ

Lesson 11 Problem Solving

Examples Directions: For items A and 1-2, choose the number sentence that shows how to solve the problem. For items B and 3-5, find the correct answer to the problem and mark the space for your choice.

A Athletic shoes normally cost $50. The price was reduced by $10. What is the new price of the shoes?

- Ⓐ $50 + $10 = ☐
- Ⓑ $10 - $50 = ☐
- Ⓒ $50 ÷ $10 = ☐
- Ⓓ $50 - $10 = ☐

B What is the cost of 6 gallons of gasoline if 1 gallon costs $1.10?

- Ⓕ $1.16
- Ⓖ $6.06
- Ⓗ $6.60
- Ⓙ Not Given

Tips

Read the question carefully. Look for key words, numbers, pictures, and figures. If necessary, work the problem on scratch paper.

Be sure to consider all the answer choices.

Practice

1 There are 24 students in a class. If they form teams of 6 students each, how many teams can they form?

- Ⓐ 24 - 6 = ☐
- Ⓑ 24 ÷ 6 = ☐
- Ⓒ 24 + 6 = ☐
- Ⓓ 24 + 64 = ☐

2 A puppy weighed 11 pounds when a family bought it. The puppy gained 5 pounds. How much does the puppy weigh now?

- Ⓕ 11 + 5 = ☐
- Ⓖ 11 x 5 = ☐
- Ⓗ 11 - 5 = ☐
- Ⓙ 5 - 11 = ☐

3 A postal worker walks 16 miles in a day. How far does the worker walk in 6 days?

- Ⓐ 12 miles
- Ⓑ 20 miles
- Ⓒ 96 miles
- Ⓓ 99 miles

4 A researcher studied 17 frogs. Eight of them were leopard frogs. How many of them were not leopard frogs?

- Ⓕ 8
- Ⓖ 9
- Ⓗ 25
- Ⓙ Not Given

5 A person earns $480 dollars a week. What else do you need to know to find out how much the person earns in an hour?

- Ⓐ How many weeks the person worked in a year
- Ⓑ How many hours the person worked in a day
- Ⓒ How much money the person earns in a day
- Ⓓ Not Given

GO

ANSWER ROWS A Ⓐ Ⓑ Ⓒ Ⓓ   1 Ⓐ Ⓑ Ⓒ Ⓓ   3 Ⓐ Ⓑ Ⓒ Ⓓ   5 Ⓐ Ⓑ Ⓒ Ⓓ
             B Ⓕ Ⓖ Ⓗ Ⓙ   2 Ⓕ Ⓖ Ⓗ Ⓙ   4 Ⓕ Ⓖ Ⓗ Ⓙ

Use this menu to answer questions 6 through 8.

KREITNER'S RESTAURANT

MegaBurger	$2.50
SuperDog	$2.25
MuchoVeggie	$2.50
Fries	$.95
Onion Rings	$1.10
Squash Chips	$.95
Cola	$.75
Lemon-Lime	$.75
Milk	$.50

6 Which of these cost the least?

- Ⓕ MegaBurger
- Ⓖ MuchoVeggie
- Ⓗ SuperDog
- Ⓙ Not Given

7 How much would a SuperDog, milk, and fries cost?

- Ⓐ $3.70
- Ⓑ $3.75
- Ⓒ $3.38
- Ⓓ Not Given

8 Which combination costs the most?

- Ⓕ MuchoVeggie and milk
- Ⓖ MuchoVeggie and cola
- Ⓗ Fries, onion rings, and milk
- Ⓙ Not Given

9 The trip from Homeville to Lincoln usually takes 25 minutes by car. While making the trip, a driver spent 12 minutes getting gas and 5 minutes waiting for a road crew. How long did it take the driver to make the trip?

- Ⓐ 32 minutes
- Ⓑ 37 minutes
- Ⓒ 48 minutes
- Ⓓ Not Given

This graph shows the amount of wood burned by several families during a winter. Study the graph, then answer numbers 10 and 11.

AMOUNT OF WOOD BURNED

Family 1	🪵🪵🪵🪵🪵🪵
Family 2	🪵🪵
Family 3	🪵🪵🪵🪵🪵🪵🪵
Family 4	🪵🪵🪵

Each 🪵 = 1 cord of wood

10 Which family used the least wood?

- Ⓕ Family 1
- Ⓖ Family 2
- Ⓗ Family 4
- Ⓙ Not Given

11 If wood costs $90 a cord, how much did Family 3 pay for wood?

- Ⓐ $270
- Ⓑ $620
- Ⓒ $630
- Ⓓ Not Given

This graph shows how much weight catfish gained each year when they were fed different diets. Study the graph, then answer numbers 12, 13, and 14.

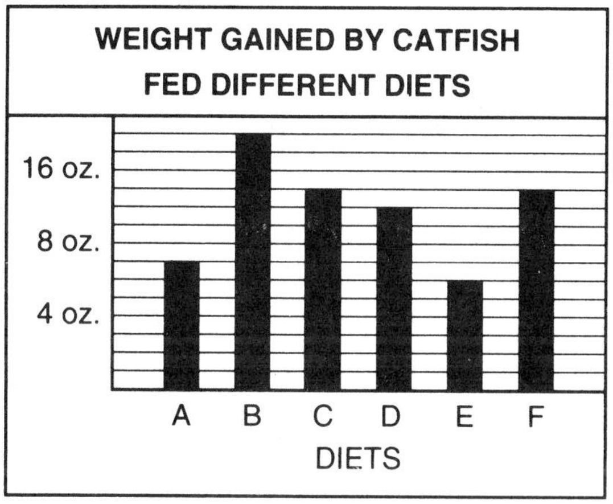

12 Which diet caused fish to gain more than a pound?

Ⓕ F
Ⓖ D
Ⓗ B
Ⓙ Not Given

13 How much did the fish gain on diet E?

Ⓐ 6 ounces
Ⓑ 8 ounces
Ⓒ 9 ounces
Ⓓ Not Given

14 Which two diets produced the same weight gains?

Ⓕ A and D
Ⓖ A and E
Ⓗ D and F
Ⓙ Not Given

15 A group of friends were waiting for a bus to ride to a movie. They knew the bus would arrive in 6 minutes. What else would they have to know to find out what time the bus was due?

Ⓐ What time the movie started.
Ⓑ What time it was now.
Ⓒ Where the bus was now.
Ⓓ Not Given

16 The price of bread was $1.29 but was increased by 8 cents. What was the new price of the bread?

Ⓕ $1.21
Ⓖ $1.36
Ⓗ $1.37
Ⓙ Not Given

17 Four families each gave $20 to a local organization for the homeless. How much money did they give all together?

Ⓐ $24
Ⓑ $60
Ⓒ $84
Ⓓ Not Given

18 The level of a pond dropped 37 inches below normal during a dry spell. It then rose 11 inches because of heavy rains. How far below normal was it?

Ⓕ 24 inches
Ⓖ 26 inches
Ⓗ 48 inches
Ⓙ Not Given

GO

ANSWER ROWS
12 Ⓕ Ⓖ Ⓗ Ⓙ 14 Ⓕ Ⓖ Ⓗ Ⓙ 16 Ⓕ Ⓖ Ⓗ Ⓙ 18 Ⓕ Ⓖ Ⓗ Ⓙ
13 Ⓐ Ⓑ Ⓒ Ⓓ 15 Ⓐ Ⓑ Ⓒ Ⓓ 17 Ⓐ Ⓑ Ⓒ Ⓓ

Lesson 11   Problem Solving

19   Sheri, Dan, and Carol each bought a snack cake for $.35. How much did they spend all together for snack cakes?

   Ⓐ $.38
   Ⓑ $1.05
   Ⓒ $1.15
   Ⓓ Not Given

20   A bus has 42 seats. Half the seats are by the window. How many seats in the bus are beside the window?

   Ⓕ 21
   Ⓖ 20
   Ⓗ 12
   Ⓙ Not Given

21   A farmer planted 18 acres on Monday, 29 on Tuesday, and 27 on Wednesday. How many acres did she plant all together?

   Ⓐ 56
   Ⓑ 64
   Ⓒ 73
   Ⓓ Not Given

22   If you knew how far it was from Boston to Phoenix and the speed of an airplane that made the trip, what information could you find?

   Ⓕ The time it took off and landed.
   Ⓖ The amount of fuel used.
   Ⓗ How long it took to fly between the cities.
   Ⓙ Not Given

This graph shows how many students used a computer and a calculator in a class each day. Each time a student used a computer or calculator, the student put a check in the correct box. Study the graph, then answer numbers 23 through 25.

	Computer	Calculator
Monday	✓✓✓✓	✓✓
Tuesday	✓✓✓	✓✓✓✓✓✓
Wednesday	✓✓✓✓✓	✓✓✓
Thursday	✓✓	✓✓✓✓✓
Friday	✓✓✓✓✓	✓✓✓✓

23   The greatest number of students who used one of the machines was on —

   Ⓐ Tuesday
   Ⓑ Wednesday
   Ⓒ Thursday
   Ⓓ Not Given

24   How many students in all used the computer?

   Ⓕ 21
   Ⓖ 20
   Ⓗ 19
   Ⓙ Not Given

25   On Thursday, how many more students used the calculator than the computer?

   Ⓐ 2
   Ⓑ 3
   Ⓒ 8
   Ⓓ Not Given

Lesson 12 Test Yourself

Examples Directions: For items E1 and 1-3, choose the umber sentence that shows how to solve each problem. For items E2 and 4-7, find the correct answer to each problem, and mark the space for your choice.

E1 A pet store owner had 18 fish. He had 3 tanks, and wanted to put the same number of fish in each tank. How many fish would he put in each tank?

- Ⓐ 18 + 3 = ☐
- Ⓑ 18 - 3 = ☐
- Ⓒ 18 ÷ 3 = ☐
- Ⓓ 18 × 3 = ☐

E2 A four-sided figure in which all the sides are equal is a _____

- Ⓕ rectangle
- Ⓖ square
- Ⓗ circle
- Ⓙ triangle

1 What is the total cost of an item if the price is $4.00 and the tax is $.24?

- Ⓐ $4 + $.24 = ☐
- Ⓑ $.24 - ☐ = $4
- Ⓒ $4 - $.24 = ☐
- Ⓓ $4 × $.24 = ☐

2 How much juice will it take to fill 10 glasses if each glass holds 8 ounces?

- Ⓕ 10 + 8 = ☐
- Ⓖ 10 - 8 = ☐
- Ⓗ 10 × 8 = ☐
- Ⓙ 10 ÷ 8 = ☐

3 A parking lot normally holds 87 cars. Because of construction, only 63 cars could fit in the lot today. How many fewer cars than normal is this?

- Ⓐ 87 + 63 = ☐
- Ⓑ 63 + 87 = ☐
- Ⓒ 63 ☐ = 87
- Ⓓ 87 - 63 = ☐

4 A square garden is 7 feet long on each side. What is the perimeter of the garden?

- Ⓕ 35 feet
- Ⓖ 28 feet
- Ⓗ 24 feet
- Ⓙ 14 feet

5 If a piece of lumber costs $2.10, how much would 4 pieces cost?

- Ⓐ $2.14
- Ⓑ $4.80
- Ⓒ $8.14
- Ⓓ $8.40

6 What time is shown on this clock?

- Ⓕ 1:55
- Ⓖ 2:55
- Ⓗ 11:02
- Ⓙ 11:10

7 After a spring storm, it took 30 hours for the snow to melt. This is —

- Ⓐ the same as a week
- Ⓑ about two days
- Ⓒ between one and two days
- Ⓓ the same as a day

ANSWER ROWS E1 Ⓐ Ⓑ Ⓒ Ⓓ   1 Ⓐ Ⓑ Ⓒ Ⓓ   3 Ⓐ Ⓑ Ⓒ Ⓓ   5 Ⓐ Ⓑ Ⓒ Ⓓ   7 Ⓐ Ⓑ Ⓒ Ⓓ
            E2 Ⓕ Ⓖ Ⓗ Ⓙ   2 Ⓕ Ⓖ Ⓗ Ⓙ   4 Ⓕ Ⓖ Ⓗ Ⓙ   6 Ⓕ Ⓖ Ⓗ Ⓙ

Lesson 12 Test Yourself

8 Which of these objects is shaped like a cube?

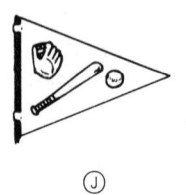

　Ⓕ　　　Ⓖ　　　Ⓗ　　　Ⓙ

9 Which of these shapes can be folded along the dotted line so the parts match?

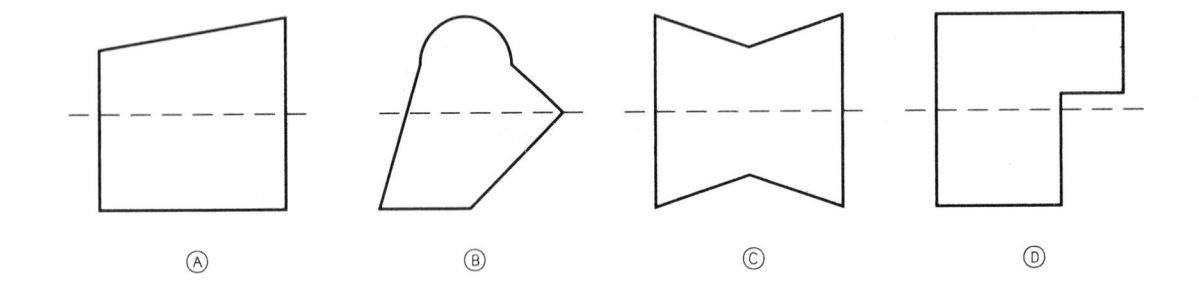

　Ⓐ　　　Ⓑ　　　Ⓒ　　　Ⓓ

10 Which statement about this pattern is true?

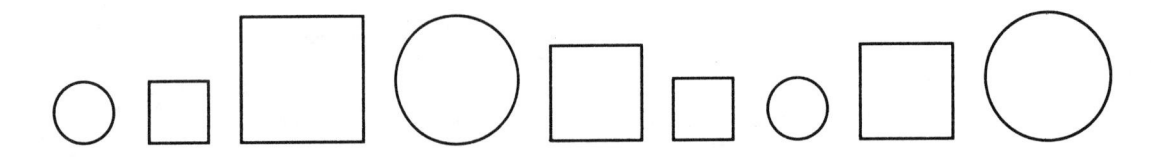

　Ⓕ There are more circles than squares.
　Ⓖ There are the same number of squares and circles.
　Ⓗ The smallest circle is always beside the largest square.
　Ⓙ The smallest circle is always beside the smallest square.

11 Which of these shapes has one more side than a square?

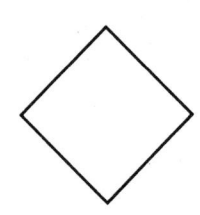

　Ⓐ　　　Ⓑ　　　Ⓒ　　　Ⓓ

126

GO

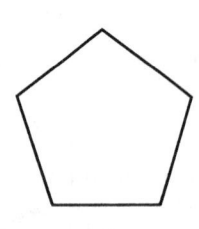

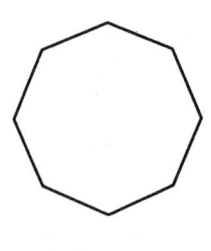

ANSWER ROWS　8 Ⓕ Ⓖ Ⓗ Ⓙ　9 Ⓐ Ⓑ Ⓒ Ⓓ　10 Ⓕ Ⓖ Ⓗ Ⓙ　11 Ⓐ Ⓑ Ⓒ Ⓓ

Study the figure below, then answer numbers 12 and 13.

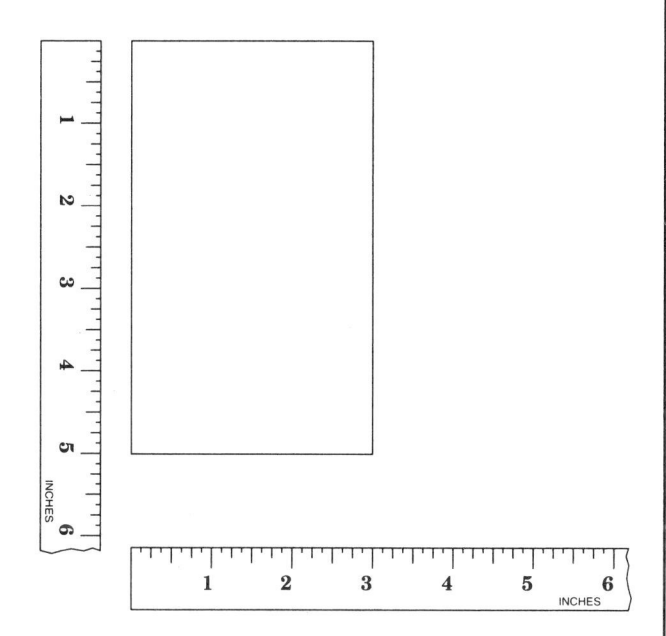

12 What is the length of the longest side of the figure?

- Ⓕ 6 inches
- Ⓖ 5 inches
- Ⓗ 3 inches
- Ⓙ 2 inches

13 The perimeter of the figure is —

- Ⓐ 16 inches
- Ⓑ 12 inches
- Ⓒ 8 inches
- Ⓓ 5 inches

14 How many quarters are in a dollar?

- Ⓕ 1
- Ⓖ 2
- Ⓗ 3
- Ⓙ 4

15 Look at the clock below. What time will it be in 40 minutes?

- Ⓐ 6:40
- Ⓑ 7:00
- Ⓒ 7:20
- Ⓓ 7:40

This graph shows the temperature measured at five different times during the day. Study the graph, then answer question 16.

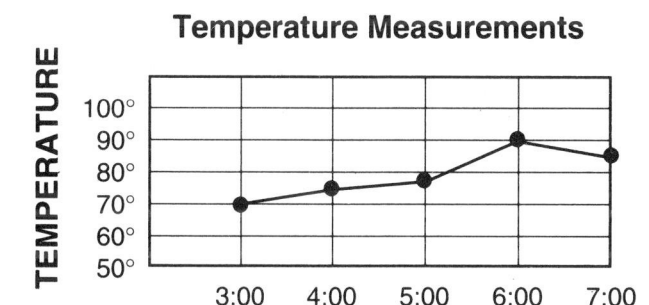

16 Based on the graph, what information cannot be found?

- Ⓕ The high temperature between 3:00 and 7:00.
- Ⓖ The low temperature between 3:00 and 7:00.
- Ⓗ The low temperature for the day.
- Ⓙ The temperature change from 3:00 to 7:00.

This graph shows the number of books read by the students in a class during a one-month period. A filled circle ● indicates a fiction book, and an empty circle ○ indicates a non-fiction book. Study the graph, then answer numbers 17 through 19.

	BOOKS READ
Natasha	○○○○○●●●
John	○○○●●●
Christopher	○●●●●●
Albert	○○○○○●●●
Nancy	○○●●●

○ = Non-Fiction
● = Fiction

17 How many books in all did Nancy read?

Ⓐ 3
Ⓑ 5
Ⓒ 8
Ⓓ 9

18 Who seems to enjoy fiction and non-fiction books about the same?

Ⓕ Natasha
Ⓖ Nancy
Ⓗ John
Ⓙ Christopher

19 How many more non-fiction than fiction books did Albert read?

Ⓐ 6
Ⓑ 5
Ⓒ 4
Ⓓ 3

20 Which of the gray shapes is congruent with the dark shape?

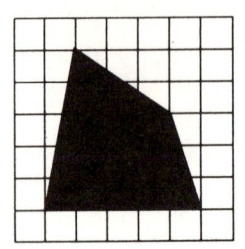

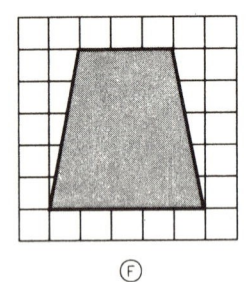

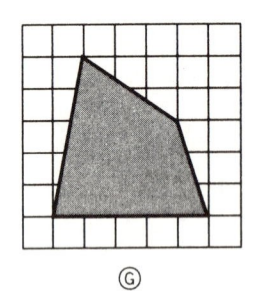

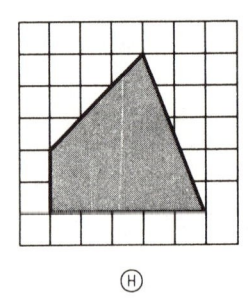

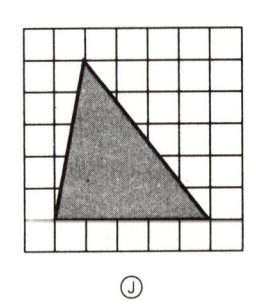

Ⓕ   Ⓖ

Ⓗ   Ⓙ

21 How much money is this?

Ⓐ $.76
Ⓑ $.61
Ⓒ $.31
Ⓓ $26

Name and Answer Sheet

To the Student:

These tests will give you a chance to put the tips you have learned to work.

A few last reminders...
- Be sure you understand all the directions before you begin each test. You may ask the teacher questions about the directions if you do not understand them.
- Work as quickly as you can during each test.
- When you change an answer, be sure to erase your first mark completely.
- You can guess at an answer or skip difficult items and go back to them later.
- Use the tips you have learned whenever you can.
- It is OK to be a little nervous. You may even do better.

Now that you have completed the lessons in this unit, you are on your way to scoring high!

PART 1 CONCEPTS

E1 Ⓐ Ⓑ Ⓒ Ⓓ	3 Ⓐ Ⓑ Ⓒ Ⓓ	7 Ⓐ Ⓑ Ⓒ Ⓓ	11 Ⓐ Ⓑ Ⓒ Ⓓ	15 Ⓐ Ⓑ Ⓒ Ⓓ	19 Ⓐ Ⓑ Ⓒ Ⓓ
E2 Ⓕ Ⓖ Ⓗ Ⓙ	4 Ⓕ Ⓖ Ⓗ Ⓙ	8 Ⓕ Ⓖ Ⓗ Ⓙ	12 Ⓕ Ⓖ Ⓗ Ⓙ	16 Ⓕ Ⓖ Ⓗ Ⓙ	20 Ⓕ Ⓖ Ⓗ Ⓙ
1 Ⓐ Ⓑ Ⓒ Ⓓ	5 Ⓐ Ⓑ Ⓒ Ⓓ	9 Ⓐ Ⓑ Ⓒ Ⓓ	13 Ⓐ Ⓑ Ⓒ Ⓓ	17 Ⓐ Ⓑ Ⓒ Ⓓ	21 Ⓐ Ⓑ Ⓒ Ⓓ
2 Ⓕ Ⓖ Ⓗ Ⓙ	6 Ⓕ Ⓖ Ⓗ Ⓙ	10 Ⓕ Ⓖ Ⓗ Ⓙ	14 Ⓕ Ⓖ Ⓗ Ⓙ	18 Ⓕ Ⓖ Ⓗ Ⓙ	

PART 2 COMPUTATION

E1 Ⓐ Ⓑ Ⓒ Ⓓ Ⓔ	3 Ⓐ Ⓑ Ⓒ Ⓓ Ⓔ	7 Ⓐ Ⓑ Ⓒ Ⓓ Ⓔ	11 Ⓐ Ⓑ Ⓒ Ⓓ Ⓔ	15 Ⓐ Ⓑ Ⓒ Ⓓ Ⓔ	19 Ⓐ Ⓑ Ⓒ Ⓓ Ⓔ
E2 Ⓕ Ⓖ Ⓗ Ⓙ Ⓚ	4 Ⓕ Ⓖ Ⓗ Ⓙ Ⓚ	8 Ⓕ Ⓖ Ⓗ Ⓙ Ⓚ	12 Ⓕ Ⓖ Ⓗ Ⓙ Ⓚ	16 Ⓕ Ⓖ Ⓗ Ⓙ Ⓚ	20 Ⓕ Ⓖ Ⓗ Ⓙ Ⓚ
1 Ⓐ Ⓑ Ⓒ Ⓓ Ⓔ	5 Ⓐ Ⓑ Ⓒ Ⓓ Ⓔ	9 Ⓐ Ⓑ Ⓒ Ⓓ Ⓔ	13 Ⓐ Ⓑ Ⓒ Ⓓ Ⓔ	17 Ⓐ Ⓑ Ⓒ Ⓓ Ⓔ	21 Ⓐ Ⓑ Ⓒ Ⓓ Ⓔ
2 Ⓕ Ⓖ Ⓗ Ⓙ Ⓚ	6 Ⓕ Ⓖ Ⓗ Ⓙ Ⓚ	10 Ⓕ Ⓖ Ⓗ Ⓙ Ⓚ	14 Ⓕ Ⓖ Ⓗ Ⓙ Ⓚ	18 Ⓕ Ⓖ Ⓗ Ⓙ Ⓚ	

PART 3 APPLICATIONS

E1 Ⓐ Ⓑ Ⓒ Ⓓ	4 Ⓕ Ⓖ Ⓗ Ⓙ	9 Ⓐ Ⓑ Ⓒ Ⓓ	14 Ⓕ Ⓖ Ⓗ Ⓙ	19 Ⓐ Ⓑ Ⓒ Ⓓ	22 Ⓕ Ⓖ Ⓗ Ⓙ
E2 Ⓕ Ⓖ Ⓗ Ⓙ	5 Ⓐ Ⓑ Ⓒ Ⓓ	10 Ⓕ Ⓖ Ⓗ Ⓙ	15 Ⓐ Ⓑ Ⓒ Ⓓ	20 Ⓕ Ⓖ Ⓗ Ⓙ	23 Ⓐ Ⓑ Ⓒ Ⓓ
1 Ⓐ Ⓑ Ⓒ Ⓓ	6 Ⓕ Ⓖ Ⓗ Ⓙ	11 Ⓐ Ⓑ Ⓒ Ⓓ	16 Ⓕ Ⓖ Ⓗ Ⓙ	21 Ⓐ Ⓑ Ⓒ Ⓓ	24 Ⓕ Ⓖ Ⓗ Ⓙ
2 Ⓕ Ⓖ Ⓗ Ⓙ	7 Ⓐ Ⓑ Ⓒ Ⓓ	12 Ⓕ Ⓖ Ⓗ Ⓙ	17 Ⓐ Ⓑ Ⓒ Ⓓ		
3 Ⓐ Ⓑ Ⓒ Ⓓ	8 Ⓕ Ⓖ Ⓗ Ⓙ	13 Ⓐ Ⓑ Ⓒ Ⓓ	18 Ⓕ Ⓖ Ⓗ Ⓙ		

UNIT 4   TEST PRACTICE

Part 1   Concepts

Examples   Directions: Find the correct answer to each problem. Mark the space for your choice.

E1

Counting by ones, what number comes after 321?

- Ⓐ 320
- Ⓑ 322
- Ⓒ 332
- Ⓓ 422

E2

How many tens are in 98?

- Ⓕ 0
- Ⓖ 6
- Ⓗ 9
- Ⓙ 10

1 How many of these numbers are less than 365?

| 329 | 265 | 429 | 502 | 456 |

- Ⓐ 2
- Ⓑ 3
- Ⓒ 4
- Ⓓ 5

2 Suppose you were the sixth person in line to get on a subway. Your friend is the eighth person in line. Which person would be between you?

- Ⓕ the ninth person
- Ⓖ the fifth person
- Ⓗ the eighth person
- Ⓙ the seventh person

3 What sign correctly completes the number sentence below?

15 ☐ 8 = 7

- Ⓐ +
- Ⓑ −
- Ⓒ ×
- Ⓓ ÷

4 Another way to write 4 × 9 is

- Ⓕ 4 + 4 + 4 + 4
- Ⓖ 4 + 9 + 4 + 9
- Ⓗ 9 + 9 + 9 + 9
- Ⓙ 9 + 4

5 In which of these must you rename a ten as ten ones or borrow a ten?

- Ⓐ 22 − 0 =
- Ⓑ 23 − 2 =
- Ⓒ 28 − 3 =
- Ⓓ 23 − 8 =

6 Which of these number lines is correct?

- Ⓕ 1 1.5 2 2.5 3 4
- Ⓖ 1 2 2.5 3 4 4.5
- Ⓗ 1 2 2.5 3 4 4.5
- Ⓙ 1 2 3 3.5 4 4.5

131 GO

Part 1   Concepts

7 Counting by threes, what comes before the number 42?

Ⓐ 40
Ⓑ 39
Ⓒ 38
Ⓓ 36

8 Which of these numbers has a 9 in the ones place and a 3 in the hundreds place?

Ⓕ 9388
Ⓖ 9839
Ⓗ 13,903
Ⓙ 19,309

9 Which numeral means forty thousand, nine hundred eight?

Ⓐ 40,908
Ⓑ 49,108
Ⓒ 400,908
Ⓓ 440,980

10 In which answer are $\frac{2}{3}$ of the circles shaded?

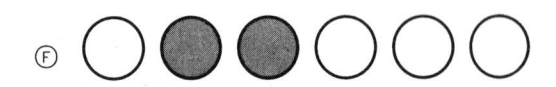

Ⓕ ○ ● ● ○ ○ ○
Ⓖ ● ● ○ ● ● ●
Ⓗ ○ ○ ○ ● ● ●
Ⓙ ● ○ ● ● ○ ●

11 What number should come next in the counting pattern below?

| 223 | 228 | 233 | 238 | |

Ⓐ 243
Ⓑ 242
Ⓒ 248
Ⓓ 253

12 What will make the number sentences below true?

$$\square + 11 = 19$$
$$22 - \square = 14$$

Ⓕ 12
Ⓖ 11
Ⓗ 9
Ⓙ 8

13 There are 27 students in a class. Each student brought in 5 insects for a science project. How can you find the number of insects they brought in all together?

Ⓐ add
Ⓑ subtract
Ⓒ multiply
Ⓓ divide

14 Which of these should you use to estimate 83 − 38 to the nearest ten?

Ⓕ 80 − 30 =
Ⓖ 80 − 40 =
Ⓗ 90 − 40 =
Ⓙ 90 − 30 =

Part 1   Concepts

15 Which of these is the same as $\frac{7}{100}$?

Ⓐ 0.7
Ⓑ 1.7
Ⓒ 0.17
Ⓓ 0.07

16 Which of these shows one more telephone than lock?

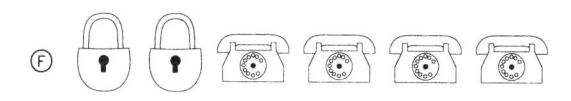

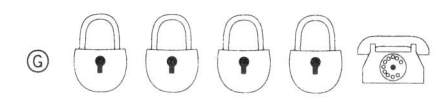

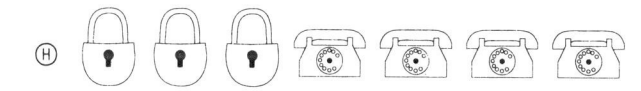

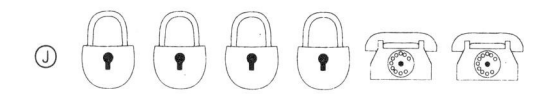

Ⓕ 🔒🔒 ☎☎☎☎
Ⓖ 🔒🔒🔒🔒 ☎
Ⓗ 🔒🔒🔒 ☎☎☎☎
Ⓙ 🔒🔒🔒🔒 ☎☎

17 Which of these is smaller than 56 and can be divided by 6?

Ⓐ 54
Ⓑ 55
Ⓒ 60
Ⓓ 64

18 If you arranged these numbers from least to greatest, which would be last?

506   521   498   152   374

Ⓕ 506
Ⓖ 498
Ⓗ 521
Ⓙ 152

19 The picture below shows a group of dogs. Some have collars, and others do not. Which of these statements is true about the dogs?

Ⓐ Fewer dogs have collars than do not.
Ⓑ More dogs have collars than do not.
Ⓒ There are a total of 8 dogs.
Ⓓ The same number of dogs have collars and do not have collars.

20 Which of these is less than $\frac{1}{6}$?

Ⓕ $\frac{1}{7}$
Ⓖ $\frac{1}{5}$
Ⓗ $\frac{2}{3}$
Ⓙ $\frac{3}{7}$

21 Look at the number sentence below. What number fits in the box to make the sentence correct?

$$1 + 6 + 7 = 10 + \square$$

Ⓐ 10
Ⓑ 9
Ⓒ 7
Ⓓ 4

Part 2 Computation

Examples — Directions: Mark the space for the correct answer to each problem. Choose "None of these" if the right answer is not given.

E1 $3\overline{)9}$
- Ⓐ 12
- Ⓑ 9
- Ⓒ 3
- Ⓓ 1
- Ⓔ None of these

E2 $12 - 8 =$
- Ⓕ 3
- Ⓖ 5
- Ⓗ 8
- Ⓙ 20
- Ⓚ None of these

1 $2 \times 7 =$
- Ⓐ 15
- Ⓑ 14
- Ⓒ 9
- Ⓓ 6
- Ⓔ None of these

2 $51 - 9$
- Ⓕ 60
- Ⓖ 44
- Ⓗ 43
- Ⓙ 32
- Ⓚ None of these

3 $12\overline{)100}$
- Ⓐ 8 R4
- Ⓑ 10
- Ⓒ 10 R4
- Ⓓ 12
- Ⓔ None of these

4 $99 + 21 + 8$
- Ⓕ 138
- Ⓖ 129
- Ⓗ 128
- Ⓙ 120
- Ⓚ None of these

5 $27 \div 9 =$
- Ⓐ 3
- Ⓑ 9
- Ⓒ 18
- Ⓓ 24
- Ⓔ None of these

6 $14 + 109 + 20$
- Ⓕ 114
- Ⓖ 129
- Ⓗ 143
- Ⓙ 144
- Ⓚ None of these

7 $11.8 - 8.2 =$
- Ⓐ 3.6
- Ⓑ 3.82
- Ⓒ 4.6
- Ⓓ 9.0
- Ⓔ None of these

8 $\$6.00 + .28 + 7.99$
- Ⓕ $12.99
- Ⓖ $13.26
- Ⓗ $13.27
- Ⓙ $13.28
- Ⓚ None of these

9 40×70
- Ⓐ 2800
- Ⓑ 2400
- Ⓒ 2040
- Ⓓ 470
- Ⓔ None of these

10 $1 - \frac{1}{2} = \square$
- Ⓕ 0
- Ⓖ $\frac{1}{4}$
- Ⓗ $\frac{1}{2}$
- Ⓙ 1
- Ⓚ None of these

Part 2   Computation

11

$\frac{3}{11} + \frac{4}{11} =$

Ⓐ $\frac{7}{11}$
Ⓑ $\frac{8}{11}$
Ⓒ $\frac{14}{15}$
Ⓓ 11
Ⓔ None of these

12

8) 63

Ⓕ 6 R3
Ⓖ 7 R6
Ⓗ 7 R7
Ⓙ 8
Ⓚ None of these

13

14 x 2 =

Ⓐ 16
Ⓑ 24
Ⓒ 26
Ⓓ 29
Ⓔ None of these

14

19 + 3 + 22 =

Ⓕ 34
Ⓖ 44
Ⓗ 46
Ⓙ 48
Ⓚ None of these

15

9) 9009

Ⓐ 100
Ⓑ 101
Ⓒ 563
Ⓓ 1001
Ⓔ None of these

16

1.3
0.22
+ 9.1

Ⓕ 10.62
Ⓖ 10.26
Ⓗ 10.13
Ⓙ 10.06
Ⓚ None of these

17

100 − 39 =

Ⓐ 17
Ⓑ 61
Ⓒ 71
Ⓓ 139
Ⓔ None of these

18

287 + 539 =

Ⓕ 826
Ⓖ 726
Ⓗ 725
Ⓙ 352
Ⓚ None of these

19

21
x 10

Ⓐ 310
Ⓑ 220
Ⓒ 210
Ⓓ 31
Ⓔ None of these

20

99 ÷ 33 =

Ⓕ 132
Ⓖ 123
Ⓗ 66
Ⓙ 3
Ⓚ None of these

21 In the table below, the numbers in Column II are 3 times larger than those in Column I. Which numbers belong in the empty spaces in the table?

Column I	Column II
9	27
10	
11	
12	36

Ⓐ 30, 31
Ⓑ 30, 32
Ⓒ 31, 33
Ⓓ 33, 34
Ⓔ None of these

Part 3 Applications

Examples Directions: For items E1 and 1-3, choose the number sentence that shows how to solve each problem. For items E2 and 4-8, find the correct answer to each problem, and mark the space for your choice.

E1 A square garden is 20 feet on each side. What is the distance around the garden?
- Ⓐ 20 + 4 = ☐
- Ⓑ 20 - 4 = ☐
- Ⓒ 20 ÷ 4 = ☐
- Ⓓ 20 x 4 = ☐

E2 About how long is a $1 bill?
- Ⓕ 6 inches
- Ⓖ 10 inches
- Ⓗ 1 foot
- Ⓙ 10 centimeters

1 A box of popcorn costs $1.25. You pay for it with 2 dollar bills. How much change will you receive?
- Ⓐ $2.00 ÷ $1.25 = ☐
- Ⓑ $1.25 + $2.00 = ☐
- Ⓒ $2.00 x $1.25 = ☐
- Ⓓ $2.00 - $1.25 = ☐

2 The temperature at 2:00 is 78°. It rises 6° by 3:00. What is the temperature at 3:00?
- Ⓕ 78 + 6 = ☐
- Ⓖ 78 - ☐ = 6
- Ⓗ 6 x ☐ = 78
- Ⓙ 78 - 6 = ☐

3 A case of juice has 24 cans. Each can holds 12 ounces of juice. How many ounces of juice are in a case?
- Ⓐ 24 ÷ 12 = ☐
- Ⓑ 24 - 12 = ☐
- Ⓒ 24 x 12 = ☐
- Ⓓ ☐ + 12 = 24

4 Scotty gets on the bus at 8:05 and arrives at school at 8:20. How long is his bus ride?
- Ⓕ 5 minutes
- Ⓖ 15 minutes
- Ⓗ 20 minutes
- Ⓙ 60 minutes

5 Jackie has 20 yards of rope she wants to be cut into 5 pieces. How long will each piece of rope be?
- Ⓐ 25 yards
- Ⓑ 7 yards
- Ⓒ 5 yards
- Ⓓ 4 yards

6 What time is shown on this clock?
- Ⓕ 8:20
- Ⓖ 3:40
- Ⓗ 3:08
- Ⓙ 8:40

7 How many quarts are in a gallon?
- Ⓐ 2
- Ⓑ 3
- Ⓒ 4
- Ⓓ 8

8 What metric unit is best to use to measure the weight of a large dog?
- Ⓕ kilometer
- Ⓖ meter
- Ⓗ gram
- Ⓙ kilogram

Use this calendar to answer questions 9 through 11.

January						
SUN	MON	TUE	WED	THU	FRI	SAT
1	2	3	4	5	6	7
8	9	10	11	12	13	14
15	16	17	18	19	20	21
22	23	24	25	26	27	28
29	30	31				

9 This calendar is for January. What day of the week was the last day in December?

Ⓐ Monday
Ⓑ Saturday
Ⓒ Sunday
Ⓓ Tuesday

10 How many Tuesdays are in January?

Ⓕ 3
Ⓖ 4
Ⓗ 5
Ⓙ 6

11 For the class trip this year, the students are going on a ski trip beginning on the third Wednesday in January and ending the following Saturday. What date will the ski trip begin?

Ⓐ January 4
Ⓑ January 25
Ⓒ January 21
Ⓓ January 18

12 A naturalist was watching the birds around a pond. Fifteen ducks were swimming in the pond when he arrived, and 8 geese landed soon afterwards. Seven cranes wandered to the pond from a nearby swamp. How many birds in all did the naturalist see?

Ⓕ 30
Ⓖ 29
Ⓗ 19
Ⓙ 15

This graph shows how long it takes students to ride the bus to school. Study the graph, then answer questions 13 and 14.

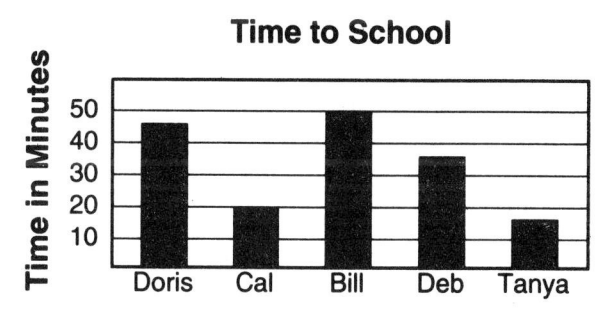

Time to School

(bar graph showing Time in Minutes: Doris ~45, Cal ~20, Bill ~50, Deb ~35, Tanya ~15)

13 Whose trip is less than half an hour?

Ⓐ Deb and Tanya
Ⓑ Doris and Bill
Ⓒ Cal and Deb
Ⓓ Cal and Tanya

14 If Bill's father drives him to school, he saves 15 minutes. How long does it take Bill to get to school if his father drives?

Ⓕ 50 minutes
Ⓖ 35 minutes
Ⓗ 25 minutes
Ⓙ 15 minutes

Part 3 Applications

The figure below shows a calculator and two metric rulers. Study the figure, then answer numbers 15 and 16.

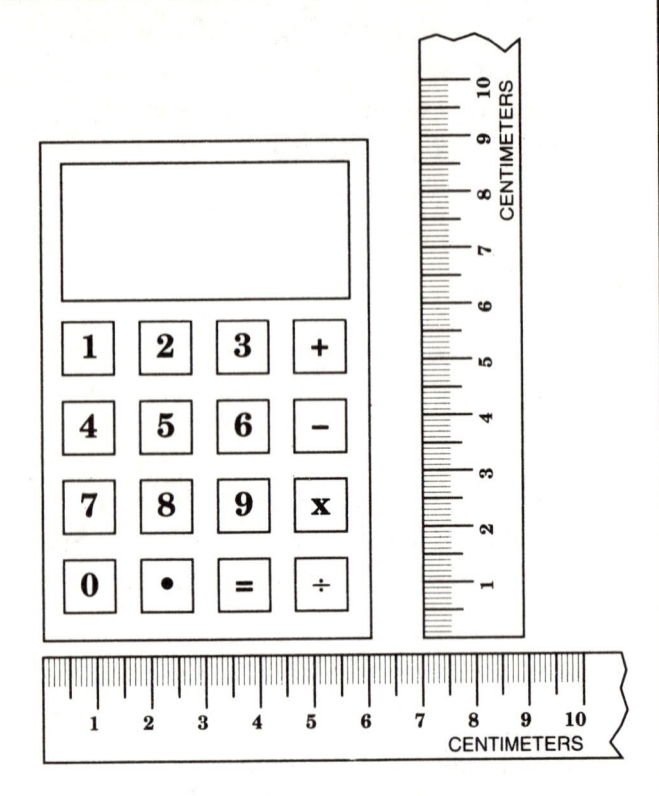

15 What are the width and length of the calculator?

Ⓐ 6 cm wide by 10 cm long
Ⓑ 6 cm wide by 9 cm long
Ⓒ 10 cm wide by 10 cm long
Ⓓ 10 cm wide by 9 cm long

16 Suppose you wanted to put colored tape around the perimeter of the calculator to decorate it. How much tape would you need?

Ⓕ 15 cm
Ⓖ 16 cm
Ⓗ 24 cm
Ⓙ 30 cm

17 Which clock shows 1:50?

Ⓐ Ⓑ Ⓒ Ⓓ

18 A gardener works for 6 hours and earns $48. Which number sentence shows how to find the amount of money the gardener earns in one hour?

Ⓕ 6 x $48 = ☐
Ⓖ $8 + ☐ = $48
Ⓗ $48 − ☐ = 6
Ⓙ 6 x ☐ = $48

19 A plane has 124 passengers. There are 3 members of the flying crew and 9 cabin attendants. How many people in all are on the plane?

Ⓐ 136
Ⓑ 135
Ⓒ 133
Ⓓ 112

Part 3   Applications

This chart shows the number of students in school. The chart shows how many students were in each grade during two different years. Study the graph, then answer numbers 20 through 22.

	1990	1991
Grade 1	52	61
Grade 2	57	59
Grade 3	54	60
Grade 4	48	55
Grade 5	47	45

20 Which grade in 1990 had the most students?

- Ⓕ Grade 1
- Ⓖ Grade 2
- Ⓗ Grade 3
- Ⓙ Grade 4

21 What was the increase in the number of students in grade 4 between 1990 and 1991?

- Ⓐ 7
- Ⓑ 6
- Ⓒ 4
- Ⓓ 3

22 What was the total number of students enrolled in grades 1, 2, and 3 in 1991?

- Ⓕ 120 students
- Ⓖ 173 students
- Ⓗ 175 students
- Ⓙ 180 students

23 Which two shapes are congruent?

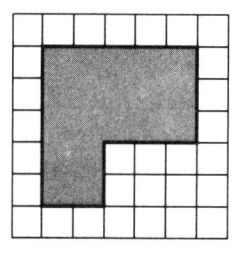

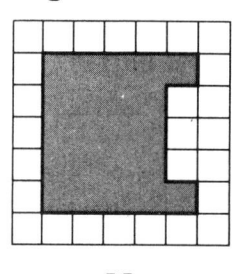

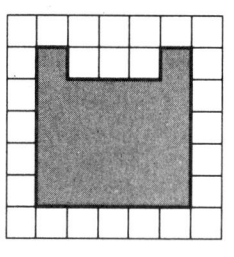

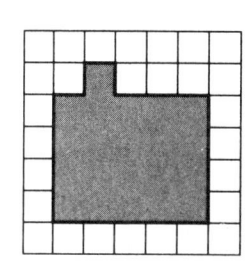

M   N

O   P

- Ⓐ M and N
- Ⓑ O and M
- Ⓒ N and O
- Ⓓ P and M

24 How much money is this?

- Ⓕ $4.70
- Ⓖ $4.87
- Ⓗ $4.97
- Ⓙ $5.07

Answer Keys

Reading Unit 1, Vocabulary

Lesson 1-pg.13
- A C
- B J
- 1 B
- 2 F
- 3 D
- 4 H
- 5 C
- 6 J
- 7 B

Lesson 2-pg.14
- A D
- B J
- 1 A
- 2 J
- 3 C
- 4 G
- 5 C
- 6 H
- 7 A

Lesson 3-pg.15
- A B
- B F
- 1 C
- 2 J
- 3 D
- 4 F
- 5 C
- 6 G
- 7 C

Lesson 4-pg.16
- A B
- B H
- 1 C
- 2 J
- 3 B
- 4 J
- 5 A

Lesson 5-pg.17
- A C
- B G
- 1 B
- 2 J
- 3 C
- 4 F
- 5 C
- 6 J

Lesson 6-pg.18-20
- E1 C
- E2 F
- E3 C
- 1 D
- 2 F
- 3 B
- 4 G
- 5 D
- 6 J
- 7 C
- 8 J
- 9 A
- 10 J
- 11 B
- 12 H
- 13 C
- 14 F
- 15 B
- 16 F
- 17 D
- 18 F
- 19 C
- 20 F
- 21 B
- 22 J
- 23 A
- 24 H
- 25 D
- 26 G
- 27 C
- 28 F

Unit 2, Reading Comprehension

Lesson 7-pg.21
- A B
- 1 A
- 2 H
- 3 D

Lesson 8-pgs.22-24
- A D
- 1 B
- 2 H
- 3 C
- 4 J
- 5 B
- 6 F
- 7 D
- 8 G

Lesson 9-pgs.25-30
- A C
- 1 B
- 2 J
- 3 A
- 4 J
- 5 B
- 6 H
- 7 C
- 8 G
- 9 D
- 10 G
- 11 D
- 12 J
- 13 D
- 14 G
- 15 D
- 16 G
- 17 A
- 18 H

Lesson 10-pgs.31-35
- E1 C
- 1 C
- 2 J
- 3 A
- 4 F
- 5 B
- 6 J
- 7 A
- 8 H
- 9 C
- 10 G
- 11 D
- 12 F
- 13 C
- 14 G
- 15 A
- 16 H

Test Practice Part 1-pgs.38-40
- E1 C
- E2 G
- E3 D
- 1 A
- 2 J
- 3 B
- 4 F
- 5 C
- 6 H
- 7 B
- 8 F
- 9 D
- 10 J
- 11 C
- 12 F
- 13 C
- 14 J
- 15 A
- 16 J
- 17 C
- 18 J
- 19 C
- 20 F
- 21 B
- 22 J
- 23 C
- 24 F
- 25 B
- 26 F
- 27 D
- 28 G

Test Practice Part 2-pgs.41-47
- E1 D
- 1 C
- 2 G
- 3 D
- 4 G
- 5 D
- 6 F
- 7 C
- 8 G
- 9 C
- 10 J
- 11 D
- 12 F
- 13 C
- 14 H
- 15 B
- 16 F
- 17 B
- 18 G
- 19 C
- 20 F
- 21 A
- 22 H
- 23 D
- 24 J

Language

Unit 1, Language Mechanics

Lesson 1-pg.49
A C
B G
1 A
2 J
3 B
4 J
5 A

Lesson 2-pg.50
A D
B G
1 A
2 J
3 B
4 F
5 B

Lesson 3-pgs.51-52
A A
B J
1 D
2 H
3 D
4 F
5 B
6 J
7 C
8 F
9 A
10 J

Lesson 4-pgs.53-55
E1 A
E2 G
1 C
2 H
3 A
4 J
5 B
6 J
7 B
8 H
9 D
10 G
11 B
12 F
13 A
14 H
15 D
16 H
17 A
18 J
19 C
20 G
21 A
22 J

Unit 2, Language Expression

Lesson 5-pgs.56-57
A B
B F
1 D
2 G
3 A
4 H
5 A
6 J
C A
D J
E B
F F
G C
7 B
8 G
9 B
10 J
11 B
12 G
13 D
14 F
15 C

Lesson 6-pg.58
A D
B F
1 C
2 G
3 A
4 H
5 D
6 F
7 C
8 J
9 C
10 G

Lesson 7-pg.59
A B
B F
1 D
2 G
3 C
4 F
5 D
6 F
7 C

Lesson 8-pgs.60-62
A A
B H
C D
1 B
2 F
3 D
4 H
5 A
6 H
7 D
8 G
9 C
10 F
11 D
12 G
13 D
14 G

Lesson 9-pgs.63-65
A B
1 D
2 H
3 D
4 G
5 C
6 J
7 A
8 G
9 A
10 H
11 D

Lesson 10-pgs.66-71
E1 B
E2 H
1 C
2 F
3 B
4 J
5 B
6 F
7 D
8 H
9 D
10 H
11 A
12 G
13 D
14 G
15 D
16 G
17 C
18 F
19 B
20 F
21 C
22 F
23 D
24 G
25 C
26 H
27 A
28 J
29 B
30 G
31 D
32 G
33 A
34 J
35 C
36 G
37 D
38 J
39 A

Unit 3, Spelling

Lesson 11-pgs.72-73
A C
B K
C B
D F
1 D
2 F
3 C
4 G
5 C
6 F
7 B
8 K
9 C
10 K
11 C
12 J
13 A
14 G
15 B
16 J
17 C
18 F
19 D
20 G
21 D
22 F
23 D
24 G

Lesson 12-pgs.74-75
E1 D
E2 G
E3 A
E4 J
1 C
2 H

141

3	A	4	F	13	B	1	C
4	J	5	B	14	J	2	F
5	B	6	J	15	A	3	D
6	J	7	D	16	H	4	J
7	A	8	H	17	B	5	D
8	H	9	A	18	F	6	F
9	E	10	J	19	B	7	C
10	G	11	B	20	G	8	G
11	D	12	F	21	C	9	D
12	G	13	B	22	H	10	F
13	D	14	H	23	A	11	C
14	J	15	D	24	H	12	H
15	B			25	B	13	D
16	F	**Unit 5, Test Practice**		26	G	14	F
17	A	**Part 1-pgs.83-85**		27	A	15	B
18	H	E1	D	28	H	16	F
19	B	E2	F	29	B		
20	J	1	A	30	H	**Math**	
21	A	2	J			**Unit 1, Concepts**	
22	G	3	B	**Test Practice**		**Lesson 1-pgs.95-96**	
23	A	4	H	**Part 3-pgs.90-91**		A	D
24	J	5	A	E1	B	B	G
25	B	6	J	E2	K	1	C
26	F	7	C	E3	C	2	F
27	B	8	F	1	D	3	B
		9	D	2	G	4	J
Unit 4, Study Skills		10	H	3	A	5	B
Lesson 13-pgs.76-78		11	D	4	J	6	G
A	C	12	H	5	B	7	A
B	F	13	A	6	F	8	J
1	B	14	G	7	C	9	C
2	J	15	B	8	H	10	F
3	A	16	J	9	A	11	D
4	G	17	D	10	G	**Lesson 2-pgs.97-98**	
5	D	18	F	11	D	A	B
6	H	19	B	12	H	B	H
7	A	20	F	13	E	1	B
8	G	21	C	14	F	2	J
9	D	22	J	15	B	3	C
10	G			16	J	4	F
11	C	**Test Practice**		17	C	5	A
12	F	**Part 2-pgs.86-89**		18	H	6	J
13	B	E1	D	19	B	7	B
14	J	E2	F	20	H	8	G
15	A	1	C	21	A	9	D
16	H	2	F	22	J	10	H
17	C	3	B	23	C	11	C
18	G	4	F	24	G	**Lesson 3-pgs.99-100**	
19	D	5	D	25	A	A	B
		6	G	26	J	B	J
Lesson 14-pgs.79-80		7	C	27	A	1	A
E1	A	8	J				
E2	H	9	A	**Test Practice**			
1	B	10	J	**Part 4-pgs.92-93**			
2	J	11	C	E1	D		
3	C	12	G	E2	G		

142

2	J	16	J	1	E	18	H
3	C	17	B	2	H	19	B
4	G	18	K	3	A	Lesson 10-pgs.117-120	
5	D	19	B	4	G	A	C
6	G	20	H	5	B	1	C
7	C	Lesson 6-pgs.106-107		6	J	2	F
8	F	A	C	7	C	3	B
9	B	B	K	8	J	4	H
10	H	1	B	9	E	5	B
11	C	2	K	10	F	6	H
Lesson 4-pgs.101-103		3	D	11	C	7	A
E1	B	4	F	12	F	8	G
E2	G	5	D	13	E	9	A
1	D	6	F	14	J	10	H
2	H	7	E	15	C	11	D
3	A	8	G	16	H	12	G
4	F	9	C	17	B	13	C
5	C	10	H	18	H	14	F
6	G	11	A	19	E	15	C
7	C	12	G	20	F	16	J
8	J	13	A	21	D	17	C
9	A	14	K	22	G	18	F
10	G	15	D	23	C	19	D
11	C	16	K	24	J	20	J
12	F	17	C	25	B	21	B
13	D	18	J	26	J	Lesson 11-pgs.121-124	
14	H	19	A	27	E	A	D
15	A	20	G	28	G	B	H
16	G	Lesson 7-pgs.108-109		29	C	1	B
17	D	A	D	30	J	2	F
18	G	B	K	31	A	3	C
19	C	1	D	32	K	4	G
20	F	2	G	33	D	5	D
Unit 2, Computation		3	C	Unit 3, Applications		6	H
Lesson 5-pgs.104-105		4	J	Lesson 9-pgs.113-116		7	A
A	B	5	A	A	D	8	G
B	K	6	G	1	C	9	D
1	A	7	E	2	F	10	G
2	H	8	J	3	B	11	C
3	B	9	D	4	J	12	H
4	J	10	F	5	B	13	A
5	E	11	B	6	F	14	J
6	F	12	H	7	D	15	B
7	C	13	C	8	H	16	H
8	G	14	F	9	B	17	D
9	D	15	B	10	F	18	G
10	K	16	G	11	C	19	B
11	B	17	D	12	G	20	F
12	F	18	K	13	D	21	D
13	D	19	D	14	G	22	H
14	J	Lesson 8-pgs.110-112		15	D	23	A
15	A	E1	B	16	F		
		E2	K	17	C		

143

24	H	16	H	10	H
25	B	17	A	11	D

Lesson 12-pgs.125-128

		18	H	12	F
E1	C	19	B	13	D
E2	G	20	F	14	G
1	A	21	D	15	B
2	H			16	J

Test Practice Part 2-pgs.134-135

3	D			17	A
4	G	E1	C	18	J
5	D	E2	K	19	A
6	F	1	B	20	G
7	C	2	K	21	A
8	F	3	A	22	J
9	C	4	H	23	C
10	J	5	A	24	G
11	B	6	H		
12	G	7	A		
13	A	8	K		
14	J	9	A		
15	B	10	H		
16	H	11	A		
17	B	12	H		
18	H	13	E		
19	D	14	G		
20	G	15	D		
21	A	16	F		

Unit 4, Test Practice Part 1-pgs.131-133

		17	B	
		18	F	
E1	B	19	C	
E2	H	20	J	
1	A	21	E	

Test Practice Part 3-pgs.136-139

2	J			
3	B			
4	H	E1	D	
5	D	E2	F	
6	H	1	D	
7	B	2	F	
8	J	3	C	
9	A	4	G	
10	J	5	D	
11	A	6	G	
12	J	7	C	
13	C	8	J	
14	G	9	B	
15	D			

Reading Progress Chart

Circle your score for each lesson. Connect your scores to see how well you are doing.

Unit 1 Lesson 1	Lesson 2	Lesson 3	Lesson 4	Unit 2 Lesson 5	Lesson 6	Lesson 7	Lesson 8	Lesson 9	Lesson 10
7	7	7		6	28			18	16
			5		27			17	15
6	6	6			26	3	8	16	14
			4	5	25			15	13
5	5	5			24		7	14	12
					23			13	11
4	4	4	3	4	22		6	12	10
					21	2		11	9
3	3	3		3	20		5	10	8
					19			9	7
			2		18			8	
2	2	2		2	17		4	7	6
					16			6	5
					15		3	5	4
1	1	1	1	1	...	1	2	3	3
							1	2	2
								1	1

145

Language Progress Chart

Circle your score for each lesson. Connect your scores to see how well you are doing.

Unit 1 Lesson 1	Lesson 2	Lesson 3	Lesson 4	Lesson 5	Unit 2 Lesson 6	Lesson 7	Lesson 8	Lesson 9	Lesson 10	Unit 3 Lesson 11	Lesson 12	Lesson 13	Lesson 14
			22						39	24	27		
			21	15			14		38	23	26	19	15
5	5	10	20	14	10		13	11	37	22	25	18	14
			19	13		7		10	36	21	24	17	13
		9	18	12	9		12		35	20	23	16	12
4	4		17	11	8	6	11	9	34	19	22	15	11
		8	16	10			10		33	18	21	14	10
		7	15		7	5		8	32	17	20	13	9
3	3		14	9	6		9	7	31	16	19	12	8
		6	13	8		4	8		30	15	18	11	7
			12	7	5		7	6	29	14	17	10	6
2	2	5	11	6	4	3	6	5	28	13	16	9	5
		4	10	5					27	12	15	8	4
		3	9	4	3	2	5	4	26	11	14	7	3
			8	3			4	3	25	10	13	6	2
	1	2	7		2		3		24	9	12	5	1
1			6	2		1		2	23	8	11	4	
		1	5	1	1		2	1	22	7	10	3	
			4				1		21	6	9	2	
			3						20	5	8	1	
			2						19	4	7		
			1						18	3	6		
									17	2	5		
									16	1	4		
									15		3		
									14		2		
									13		1		
									12				
									11				
									10				
									9				
									8				
									7				
									6				
									5				
									4				
									3				
									2				
									1				

146

Math Progress Chart

Circle your score for each lesson. Connect your scores to see how well you are doing.

Unit 1 Lesson 1	Lesson 2	Lesson 3	Unit 2 Lesson 4	Lesson 5	Lesson 6	Lesson 7	Unit 3 Lesson 8	Lesson 9	Unit 4 Lesson 10	Lesson 11	Lesson 12
11	11	11	20	20	20	19	33	19	21	25	21
10	10	10	19	19	19	18	32	18	20	24	20
9	9	9	18	18	18	17	31	17	19	23	19
8	8	8	17	17	17	16	30	16	18	22	18
7	7	7	16	16	16	15	29	15	17	21	17
6	6	6	15	15	15	14	28	14	16	20	16
5	5	5	14	14	14	13	27	13	15	19	15
4	4	4	13	13	13	12	26	12	14	18	14
3	3	3	12	12	12	11	25	11	13	17	13
2	2	2	11	11	11	10	24	10	12	16	12
1	1	1	10	10	10	9	23	9	11	15	11
			9	9	9	8	22	8	10	14	10
			8	8	8	7	21	7	9	13	9
			7	7	7	6	20	6	8	12	8
			6	6	6	5	19	5	7	11	7
			5	5	5	4	18	4	6	10	6
			4	4	4	3	17	3	5	9	5
			3	3	3	2	16	2	4	8	4
			2	2	2	1	15	1	3	7	3
			1	1	1		14		2	6	2
							13		1	5	1
							12			4	
							11			3	
							10			2	
							9			1	
							8				
							7				
							6				
							5				
							4				
							3				
							2				
							1				

Student Notes

Student Notes

Student Notes

Student Notes

Student Notes

Student Notes